POLLY PRY
The Woman Who Wrote the West

JULIA BRICKLIN

TWODOT®

GUILFORD, CONNECTICUT
HELENA, MONTANA

A · TWODOT® · BOOK

An imprint and registered trademark of The Rowman & Littlefield Publishing Group, Inc.
4501 Forbes Blvd., Ste. 200, Lanham, MD 20706
www.rowman.com

Distributed by NATIONAL BOOK NETWORK

Copyright © 2018 by Julia Bricklin

British Library Cataloguing in Publication Information available

Library of Congress Cataloging-in-Publication Data available

ISBN 978-1-4930-3439-0 (hardcover)
ISBN 978-1-4930-3440-6 (e-book)

♾™ The paper used in this publication meets the minimum requirements of American National Standard for Information Sciences—Permanence of Paper for Printed Library Materials, ANSI/ NISO Z39.48-1992.

Printed in the United States of America

CONTENTS

I would like to express my gratitude to the following people:

Sarah C. Smith, Abby Hoverstock, Coi Drummond-Gehrig, Eve M. Faris, Andi Pusavat, Mark Bricklin, Madison S. Bricklin, Ellen Grim, Michael Scheuchl, Linda Klibanow, Susie Greenberg, Richard Greenberg, Kate Greenberg, Marian Greenberg Quinn, Josh Sides, Teri Taylor Hinson, Brenda Himelfarb, Susie Brown Thomas, Carol Dozier, and Jennifer Jung-Kim. As always, thank you to Kevin, Jane, and Andrew Bricklin.

Special thanks to the Denver Public Library, Western History and Genealogy Department.

Author's Note

Michael Bujega, who teaches journalism at Iowa State University, once defined objectivity as "seeing the world as it is, not how you wish it were." It could be said that newswoman Leonel Ross Campbell Anthony O'Bryan, "Polly Pry," did both. She was rarely surprised by facts she learned, because for the most part, she only gathered facts that supported her worldview. And often, her facts were not so much truths as they were opinions, carefully elicited from people who supported her stance or even just her own conclusions.

But with a few notable exceptions, objectivity was not a journalistic goal of most American newspapers until the 1920s. In the latter part of the nineteenth century, journalists talked about something called "realism" rather than objectivity. This was the idea that if reporters simply dug out the facts and ordered them together, truth would reveal itself rather naturally. In Campbell's case, she usually dug out only the facts that seemed pertinent to the way she wished to shape a story.

But often the stories Polly Pry wrote were ones that had never been investigated before—certainly not by a woman, and particularly not by a woman who lived in the West. At the turn of the nineteenth century into the twentieth, Denver was a city in flux, attempting to define itself economically, politically, and socially. The incredible wealth generated by silver mining, land speculation, and manufacturing in post–Civil War Colorado spurred a tidal wave of population growth that brought problems with it, including an increase in density and housing shortages, as well as growing resentment of immigrant labor. The infusion of new life was attended by all the contrasts of a boom-town atmosphere: Denver sprawled haphazardly in all directions, "a city of broad streets and squalid slums; of dives and churches, of *nouveaux riches* and of college men." When Leonel arrived in 1898, Denver's government was a model of impotency: disorganization was exacerbated by an entrenched bureaucracy, looting of public moneys went noticed but uncorrected, and graft and vote fraud were common features of the administration. And for all of its resources, Denver (and portions of Colorado at large) struggled to find the best way to care for its poor, its veterans, its sick, and its orphans. In other words, "Polly Pry" had a lot of material to work with.

This is not to say that Campbell was wholly original by investigating the plight of those who struggled during the Progressive Era. Her career began in the last decade of the nineteenth century at the height of the circulation wars between Joseph Pulitzer and William Randolph Hearst. The war between those two titans to gain the hearts and minds (and dollars) of American readers spurred them to try stunts like sending a woman undercover into a New York City insane asylum to report on conditions there, as Pulitzer did with Elizabeth Cochrane, aka Nellie Bly. There is no question Polly Pry emulated Cochrane's success in this regard, following suit with her own investigations into Indian schools, asylums, and hospitals, albeit in Colorado. A dozen years after Cochrane famously went "around the world in 72 days" alone to report on exotic locales for readers at home, Polly Pry did similarly by reporting unchaperoned from Europe. Both women even spent considerable time in Mexico at roughly the same time, writing voluminous material about their observations.

But Campbell was unique in that she saw the "big picture," showing her readers how a politician's failure to pass a piece of legislation or his looting of public funds could ultimately impact his constituents. She warned her readers that they, too, could find themselves in a similar situation as alleged murderers Alfred Packer, or Tom Horn, if they did not hold their lawmakers and judges accountable by taking the time to review the facts of a case. She even took issue with suffrage, arguing in the press with well-known female reformers in the press about the best way to further a woman's voice in local politics.

When reading this book, one might be jarred by some of the racial slurs and attitudes expressed in Campbell's writing. These are reflective of the times in which Campbell lived and should be read within the context of prevailing notions of the early twentieth century, though her style and opinions were her own. One might also be taken aback by seemingly libelous or slanderous language that would not be tolerated in respectable newspapers in modern times and would probably be subject to lawsuits today—again, passages containing this language should be read within the context of what were different legal constraints in early twentieth-century

America. In some cases, I edited quotes so the passages can be free of the flowery, run-on prose that was a popular style during Campbell's career, but which is difficult to read today. And though Leonel Ross Campbell often went by "Mrs. Anthony" or "Mrs. O'Bryan" depending on whom she was married to at the time, I use "Campbell"—her maiden name—throughout the book for simplicity's sake.

INTRODUCTION

At eight o'clock in the evening of January 10, 1904, the doorbell rang at 131 West Colfax Avenue. It was an exceptionally clear night in Denver, with no rain, no snow. But it was below freezing—about twenty-five degrees—and although she was not expecting any more party guests, Leonel Ross Campbell did not feel right about leaving the doorbell ringer outside. "Look out," a friend cautioned her as she passed from the kitchen through the living room, "you want to be careful." Campbell, better known as the journalist "Polly Pry," cautiously opened the door while pressing herself parallel to the wall behind it. With that opening, two shots rang out. "I saw a long red flame, caught a fleeting glimpse of a big man in dark clothes, and a derby hat," she later recalled. One bullet splinter cracked the heavy oak doorframe, and the other went wide of any mark.[1]

Neither bullet hit Campbell, and the would-be assassin fled into the night as she screamed. Friends rushed to make sure she was not hurt, while one rang for the police. Campbell then rushed out to see if she could catch a glimpse of the man, but he was long gone. She remembered uncertainly that he had a dark moustache and "a side face marred by a red mark." The next day, all of Denver rallied to Campbell's side. The chief of police announced: "They certainly intended to kill her. We have men out West who would be willing to kill her or any newspaper man for the asking." The governor offered to call out the militia to guard her; newsboys set up a sentry around her house.[2]

And yet, this was not the first time someone fired bullets at a conspicuous target like Leonel Ross Campbell. Just a few years earlier, not long after arriving in Denver, she had flung herself in front of her new bosses, the owners of the *Denver Post*, to save them from the gunshots of an irate attorney who accused them and Campbell of interfering with the defense of his client. According to the *Post*, William W. Anderson, counsel for alleged cannibal Alfred Packer, charged into the offices of Harry Heye Tammen and Frederick Gilmer Bonfils on January 13, 1900, at noon.

He lobbed heated accusations against Tammen and Bonfils. Anderson, dubbed "Plug Hat" by local citizenry for his fancy felt toppers, left but returned shortly with a revolver and shot each newspaperman twice, though neither one fatally. In the weeks and months following, and especially when the *Post* reported on Anderson's trial proceedings in April, the story was embellished to include Campbell as Tammen's savior:

> *Mrs. [Campbell] Anthony, who had gone to the window to scream for help, found it locked and as quickly as possible she ran to Mr. Tammen's assistance, and got there as the last shot was fired. She placed herself between the body of Mr. Tammen and his assailant, begging and imploring Mr. Anderson not to shoot again. Mr. Anderson did not heed her prayer, but aimed the gun first on one side of her and then the other, she following the direction of the pistol, swaying her body back and forth to keep herself between the weapon and Mr. Tammen, all the while imploring Mr. Anderson not to shoot again. She so successfully foiled him in his attempt that he desisted, and finally left the room and the premises, going out by the way of the side door upon Curtis street.*[3]

In a later account, employees of the *Post* elaborated further. They overheard Campbell do more than just plead with ol' Plug Hat. She purportedly grabbed the barrel of Anderson's gun, and when he threatened to kill her, she replied, "Go ahead! And then *hang.*"[4] Packer himself was called in to testify about his power-of-attorney relationship with Anderson; the jury could not come to an agreement about whether the attorney had planned to murder, and so he was found not guilty.

Why would such a refined woman as Campbell—often described as "gorgeous," "regal," "intrepid," and "clever"—find herself in predicaments where her life was in danger? Temperament, no doubt, but also the lack of a roadmap. There were not many professions for an extremely intelligent woman like Campbell in the early nineteenth century, especially if she came from ordinary stock. More specifically, there were not many opportunities for adventurous and assertive wives and daughters to earn their own paychecks, and so a rarity like Campbell had to create her own position. She took it upon herself to become a hard-charging journalist, exposing the rotten underbelly of Denver's Democratic Party machine during the first decades of the twentieth century, and also social injustices in neighboring states and even Mexico. Campbell aimed her sharp pen at gambling dens, prostitution, drinking, bribery, graft, and in particular, the American Federation of Labor in the Mile High City. This left her vulnerable to those who felt they had been wronged in print.

At the turn of the twentieth century, when communication throughout the West was slow and limited, locally published newspapers and periodicals were more influential than they are today. Although men controlled the vast majority of these publications, some women also found their way into publishing. As Polly Pry, Campbell was the *Denver Post*'s first female reporter and one of its most colorful ones.[5] In 1901, she singlehandedly campaigned to prevail upon the governor to parole the notorious Packer, who had served more than half of his forty-year sentence. After succeeding at this, Polly Pry launched an investigation of the mineworkers' labor struggle in Telluride. When the union boycotted the *Post*, the paper refused to stand behind her and she left shortly after that to start her own weekly magazine.

Polly Pry, Campbell's eponymous paper, lasted only two years. During that run, it reported every minute detail of the burgeoning social scene of Denver and Arapahoe Counties. More incisively, it reported on uniquely local political issues. For instance, Campbell noted, "The men responsible for open and unbridled gambling in Denver are the merchants, saloon-keepers and owners of property within the red light district . . . Probably fifteen percent of their rakings is ladled out for official protection. The city gets none of it. Part goes to the political party in power for campaign purposes, and part, $60,000 per annum, to certain gentlemen at the city hall."[6]

Polly Pry belonged to a line of even more famous women journalists that included reform-minded investigators like Ida Tarbell and Elizabeth Cochrane, also known as Nellie Bly. These women, in turn, had followed a path laid for them by antebellum and post-Civil War scribes such as Margaret Fuller, Jane Cunningham Croly, and the first female African-American newspaper editor Mary Ann Shadd Cary. There were also quite a few "sob sisters" who, when Campbell's nom-de-plume was becoming famous, were appealing to readers' sympathies with their accounts of tenement fires and wayward children. Dorothy Dix (Elizabeth Meriwether Gilmer), Annie Laurie (Winifred Black), and Ada Patterson were household names at roughly the same time as Campbell. Polly Pry was different. She scorned "sob stories" after a year or two of writing them, and instead focused mostly on long-term political and social issues that would shape Denver and other parts of the West.

Campbell was sometimes ambivalent and hypocritical. For example, in print, she thoroughly and cruelly denigrated philanthropist Margaret Tobin Brown, "The Unsinkable Molly Brown," as the worst kind of social climber, but then forged a close friendship with her based on a mutual interest in women's suffrage and the hardships endured by mining families. Her printed observations about the Denver social scene were rife with barbed observations of others' personal lives, even while her own rivaled them in shame. "Among the gentlemen who took advantage of the dense crowd to take to the show other than their lawfully wedded spouses were a prominent attorney, a real estate man and a well-known physician," she wrote in *Polly Pry*.[7] In truth, Campbell's own marital record was disastrous—both of her ex-husbands were alcoholics and philanderers, and both spent much more money than they earned. Additionally, Campbell's immediate family, including her siblings, suffered indignities that were kept private: infidelity, child abandonment, financial difficulty.

But Campbell's worst transgression was against truth, astonishing given the thousands of pages of detailed, insightful, and passionate pieces she wrote about people and places in the American West and around the world. Her offense was that much of her early work was complete fiction. "She was full of beans," said one biographer. And she was. She did *not* go to the Philippines in 1899 and cover atrocities against Americans and "Insurrectos"—although she did write illuminating pieces about that experience, and about the very real effects of what is now referred to as post-traumatic stress disorder. And Polly Pry did *not* embark upon a five-month sojourn to Europe in 1900 to write about the beatification of Pope Leo XIII in Rome, Antwerp's art treasures, and "the dark side of Paris life," though she did craft together a written experience about those places that her readers would never forget. To be sure, Campbell traveled more widely than the average woman during her lifetime.

There is no doubt that Campbell—sometimes referred to as "Nell"—had a talent for description and scene setting. She purportedly traveled to New York's Chinatown to report on the death of a white woman who had stabbed herself after learning that her son by a Chinese man had died in a fall from a tenement. Here she described her entry into the tenement:

> *I shuddered as I climbed the broken steps and entered the dark hall where the faint light from the halls above struggled with the thick blackness of the place. Shadowy figures huddled about the lower step, but as I approached they drew back into the darkness, where I could not see them but could hear their breathing and feel their eyes upon me. Above, the wailing cries grew louder and indistinct voices floated down towards me. I stumbled against something on the stairs and hurriedly crossed myself, when I bent down and looked into the bead-like eyes of an old man who crouched there in the gloom, an old man with toothless mouth, scant gray queue and ugly, claw-like fingers. . . . All the other doors are open and the place swarms with men and women, with here and there a little child clinging to its mother's dress and staring with frightened eyes at the dread policeman.[8]*

And yet, Campbell redeemed herself. These "travels" to bigger American cities and Europe established her financially and professionally enough to report credibly on the events affecting Colorado and the West in general during the tumultuous early decades of the twentieth century. She developed a passion for demanding justice and pointing out political hypocrisy that was unmatched by other reporters in the region. Those who wasted citizens' money were regularly in the reporter's crosshairs:

> *Here in Denver we have five district judges, and if an important case comes up not one of these five judges seems able to dispose of the same, but shirks the responsibility by calling an outside judge to hear it, or the case is sent to some other county with all its attendant costs and expenses.[9]*

The fortunes of great families—the Guggenheims, Rockefellers, and Goulds—were built in part on the valuable ores that lay under the Colorado soil, and Campbell was determined to show the world how greed and the push for frontier freedom bred violence from both labor and capital. In both the *Denver Post* and her own publication *Polly Pry* a few years later, Campbell devoted dozens of pages to the mining wars in Las Animas County, and a running word war with Big Bill Haywood and Charles H. Moyer and other labor leaders. She brutally defamed Mary "Mother Jones" Harris, even going so far as to claim that the union organizer had once owned a brothel.

Polly Pry also wrote about what she considered heinous government behavior in other western states as well as in Mexico. For example, she wrote both columns and plays about the Brownsville Affair of 1906 in Texas, where black soldiers were falsely accused of shooting a white bartender, and of "the cowardice" of President Theodore Roosevelt, who ordered the soldiers dishonorably discharged. Polly covered the events surrounding the arrest and trial of Tom Horn, the notorious hired gunman believed to have killed more than seventeen people, including the teenaged son of a Wyoming sheep rancher who was feuding with a neighbor over livestock lands. Campbell pointed out that Horn, who was convicted, rightfully deserved the wrath of Wyoming's residents, but that the authorities in that state should have also prosecuted the cattle barons who had hired Horn. "When is 5 Cents Worth $12,000?" she asked in one headline, referring to the fact that when Tom Horn was arrested, he had five pennies to his name, and that John Coble and his associates quickly put up thousands for Horn's defense, showing their own culpability. And nobody could match Campbell's exploits in border towns such as Juarez, where she followed Pancho Villa around in 1914, deftly reporting on the trail of terror left by the revolutionary hero.

Leonel Ross Campbell Anthony O'Bryan, alias Polly Pry, was an adventuress, labor activist, suffragette, and dramatist, and above all, a woman who did not let danger get in the way of a good story. At first, she used trickery and her wits to establish her career in Denver. But she became an incisive and thorough journalist, taking sometimes unpopular stances in Colorado's rough-and-tumble system of politics and, more generally, social injustices in the West. Later in life, though she had no children of her own, she worked tirelessly as an officer with the Red Cross to help orphans in war-torn Europe during and after World War I, and also those at home who were victims of poverty, especially that caused by labor wars in mining towns like Cripple Creek and Goldfield: "The woman in the home looks up, and out of its black depths reads winter hardships, deprivations, cold, hunger, disease, and perhaps death for the little ones playing so heedlessly in the sunshine to-day, and grows sick and cold with a haunting dread."[10] Above all, Polly Pry showed that a woman wielding a pen could shape the West as well as any man holding a gun.

CHAPTER I

Old Mexico, New York

On a sweltering hot day in August of 1869, Nelson James Campbell thought he had figured out a way to buy his own house. The carpenter was making repairs on an old tavern in Henderson, Illinois, along with his friend Frank Jones, a plasterer. Wrenching down some termite-infested rafters, the two found a large, oblong box, securely fastened with a lock. With some difficulty, they got the box down, broke it open, and found a mess of glittering gold coins. They could hardly believe their good luck, and congratulated each other—surely no one else could claim the treasure, as the structure had been vacant for years.

Campbell's thrill was short-lived. He and Jones gave the coins to a local bank inspector to assess their value. After performing various tests, the cashier deemed them completely worthless fakes. It appeared that the hermit-like men who had lived in the tavern during the Civil War had been exceptionally good counterfeiters. Campbell was inconsolable, believing the heavens had singled him out to be cheated and wronged.

While he eventually got over this slight by the hand of fate, Nelson Campbell had good reason to feel that disappointment was always around the corner for him. He was born in 1831, in New York, to Sarah Elizabeth Johnson and Jessie Campbell. Jessie died in 1835, and Sarah married well-to-do farmer Joseph Catlin less than a year later. But Catlin had already had two wives before Sarah, and he already had sired thirteen children—he would have two more with Sarah. There was no room or extra food for Nelson, so in his mid-teens, he joined thousands of other young men in laying down track through the Panamanian jungle, building a railroad to cross the isthmus. The wages were good enough to risk getting malaria or dysentery, and when the line was completed in 1855, Nelson soon found a job in central Illinois. Here, he met his wife.

Mary Elizabeth McKinney was born in Christian County, Kentucky, to John and Temperance "Tempy" McKinney, in 1838. Mary's birth coincided with the US removal of indigenous Osage Indians from southwestern Missouri to Kansas Territory, along with transplanted Kickapoos, Delawares, and Shawnees. Ten years later, with white settlement underway, Mary's parents moved her and her three brothers to Jasper, Missouri, where John had purchased more than 1,600 acres of prime corn farming land, and there, the McKinneys had four more children.

Although John McKinney undoubtedly owned slaves, he leaned away from secession like others in the hamlet of Medoc. Hardly a political lightning rod, McKinney was shot and killed in his own home on June 10, 1862. His murderer could have been a staunchly Confederate neighbor in Saroxie or Carthage, or a Union guerilla from Kansas, or simply a hungry transient.

Mary got word of her father's death while mourning a stillborn son—her third birth. How she met the father of her children, Nelson Campbell, is anybody's guess, but the pair had married on January 31, 1856, in Clinton, DeWitt County, Illinois. Campbell worked as a framer at a carriage factory, and eventually bought some acreage in nearby Texas Township. The family was almost certainly a fixture at Cumberland Presbyterian, the first church built in the county. It is entirely possible that the Campbells passed Abraham Lincoln on the road or in town. The future president kept a law office in Clinton until 1859, and his partner, Clifton Moore, was a member of their church.

Leonel Ross Campbell, called Nell by her family, was born in Clinton on November 27, 1859, a date that would vary as much as eleven years when Nell tried to appear younger later on. Mary and Nelson were overjoyed to have a little girl to keep two-year-old Charles company, and they lived comfortably, if sparsely, in a one-story frame house on their property, with dozens of pigs and goats to chase in the yard.

In the summer of 1863, when Leonel was four, Nelson reported to the provost marshal for Civil War service. It is not clear to what regiment he was assigned—in all probability, it would have been the 107th—but in any event, he did not see combat. All the same, the Campbells' farm foundered, as did most in Dewitt County, owing to the scarcity of able-bodied workers. And so, in 1866, Leonel's family packed up all their belong-ings and moved 150 miles south to Decatur, where Nelson's stepfather begrudgingly rented him some rooms in his large farmhouse.

Mary gave birth to Leonel's brother, Alonzo, a month after Nelson's worthless windfall of gold coins, in the autumn of 1869. Nelson worked hard in Decatur, and when a direct railroad line opened up from the hamlet to the vibrant city of St. Louis in 1871, he was one of the first passengers to make regular forays there for better wages. He promptly moved his family to St. Louis, where he missed the wide expanse of farmland in Decatur but not the claustrophobic feel of his stepfather's silent judgment. Nelson even managed to save some money during the depression that started with the Panic of 1873, working on projects like the Eads Bridge, before all of the city works projects dried up eighteen months later.

Leonel entered her teen years in St. Louis with some shenanigans, according to many sources. The historian Barbara Belford notes that she was sent to private boarding school when she was fifteen, where she grew bored and restless, and found a way to escape. Her escape hatch was George Henry Anthony Jr., a wealthy Kansas engineer who was building the Mexican Central Railroad and one night in 1874 or 1875, she put on a long dress made of black velvet, climbed over the school wall, and eloped with him. Very quickly, the young woman found herself left to her own devices in a steamy hotel room on the dry and desolate border between the United States and Mexico:

> *I was a bride of only a few days' standing when I arrived in El Paso . . . my better half . . . had been compelled to hurry back to his post. Rooms had been prepared for us at the hotel, but when that first hot night I was discovered, about midnight, seated, á la Turk, on the top of a center table, with the tears streaming down my cheeks and the whole place reeking with the suffocating odor of pennyroyal, of which I had used a quart, I was simply bundled into a carriage and taken over to the private car, where I lived for many long days before I could be persuaded to return to my rooms where the fleas had so completely routed me.[1]*

Except, this did not happen. At least, not when Nell was fifteen years old. Or even twenty. Campbell and Anthony did not meet until the summer of 1883, when she was twenty-four and he was twenty-seven.

While Anthony was not the much older paramour depicted in the scant stories about this time in Campbell's life, the love affair when it did occur was scandalous for another reason: he had just deserted his wife and their two young daughters. George Henry Anthony Jr. had married Emma Putnam in August 1873, when he was only nineteen and his bride eighteen. They had a daughter, Anna Elizabeth, exactly a year later, and Alma four years after that. Anthony was able to create a very comfortable life for his family, as he was the son of Kansas's seventh governor and, as such, received coveted governmental jobs.

In 1883, Anthony Jr. replaced a well-respected gentleman as chief clerk of the Leavenworth penitentiary. The *Leavenworth Times* noted that the young Anthony, son of "his majesty's excellency," was a "mere youth" and not a proper person for the position. "It is no boy's play," continued the paper, "and to take away a man of experience and judgment and put in a white-headed boy seems like folly."[2] Folly or not, it was not the first and certainly not the last time the younger Anthony obtained plum assignments because of his father's influence.

Like most Victorian women, Emma Putnam Anthony did not take her marriage vows lightly. The Anthony family was highly respected. Before he became governor of Kansas, the senior Anthony was a highly decorated Civil War veteran, proprietor and editor of the *Kansas Farmer*, assistant assessor of the US Internal Revenue Service, and president of the Kansas State Board of Agriculture. His cousin was Daniel Read ("D. R.") Anthony, owner of the *Leavenworth Times*, and D. R.'s sister was the formidable suffragette, Susan B. Anthony. Emma enjoyed the social status this family conferred. Besides that, she was completely in love with the dashing junior Anthony, with his quick wit, devil-may-care attitude, green eyes and shock of dark, lustrous black hair that was almost blue and matched by the long walrus moustache that was so fashionable at the time.

But Anthony Jr. took his marriage less seriously than Emma—at least at that time. He was young, and entitled, and adventure beckoned when his father offered any management position that looked interesting at any given time. He spent little time at home. When he married Emma in 1873, he was a newly installed deputy tax collector for the Internal Revenue Service, responsible for the eastern half of Kansas. In 1877, his father gave him a commission as a notary public for the county of Leavenworth, and also the penitentiary job.[3] Local papers noted how Junior took advantage of his positions, such as not paying for his cigar orders from various shops and selling untaxed whiskey that he had confiscated at state fairs.[4]

Emma finally filed for divorce, citing "abandonment." Less than three months later, on July 30, 1883, Leonel Ross Campbell and George Henry Anthony Jr. wed in St. Louis. Campbell never spoke of how they met. Perhaps he came into Byron Nugent Dry Goods, where she worked as a saleslady. The *St. Louis Post Democrat* took note of the nuptials, and queried the officiant, who described the affair as rather strange:

> *I was somewhere about the church last Monday, when a young man stepped up to me and asked if I was Rev. Mr. Adams. I told him I was. He then said there were a couple who wanted to be married waiting at my house for me. I walked over to the house and there met a party of four or five very well dressed, pleasant looking people. I did not know any of them, and I confess I was a little surprised at the wedding party, as they all looked to be wealthy people—people who would make a display of a wedding. The bride and groom were [a] handsome, sensible couple.[5]*

The reverend asked no questions, as the legal requirements for marriage appeared in order and they seemed to know what they were doing. When the reporter asked a friend of Anthony's what he thought of the proceeding, he said he could not speculate, but of course he did, pointing out that there seemed to be "an element of romance" in the marriage, hinting that it was hasty. "It would be interesting to know," the *Post Democrat* continued, "why the scion of such a distinguished family as Governor Anthony's should carry off a St. Louis young lady in so quiet a manner."[6]

Whatever the circumstances of their meeting and marriage, it would be hard for any young man not to be attracted to Leonel. She was five foot five, with alabaster skin and a mouth that was not tiny but was perfectly proportioned. She had truly ash blonde, long hair that twisted naturally into shiny curls. Her jaw line was just a bit square and her eyes just a tad inset—almost like a Siamese cat's—but the largeness and blueness of those eyes offset any hint of masculinity and gave her an extraordinarily interesting look.

In lieu of a honeymoon, the Anthonys made their way from St. Louis to El Paso by way of the Atchison, Topeka, and Santa Fe rail line, marveling at the grandeur of the chasms of the Royal Gorge near Cañon City, Colorado, as they sped by. A fellow passenger, the adventurer Edwin Everett and his touring company invited the bridal party to dine with them before the couple had to disembark in Texas and then make their way into Chihuahuha, Mexico.[7] Campbell observed that the heat began to pick up precipitously as they neared New Mexico:

> *All day we had rushed along past great sand plains, through tiny mud-colored villages, overdry streams, up rocky heights and down into horrible valleys, where the wind blew straight from the bottomless pit—hot, suffocating and laden with dust. Long before noon we had shed the last garment that could decently be parted with, and, fan in hand, lay back in our chairs and sighed for the night and a cessation of the dazzling light of the great, blazing sun which had so mercilessly pursued us since early morning, and of the withering heat which was slowly reducing us to a liquid state.*

At last they reached El Paso, but Campbell was disappointed at what she saw:

> *I scrambled into my discarded garments, and, leaning on the rear platform of our car, gazed with sinking heart at the unspeakably dreary prospect before me . . . A narrow valley, hemmed in by great sun-baked hills that rose one above another until they melted in the distant mountains, a tiny river that on one occasion can be a roaring torrent meandered along one side, fringed with a scraggling row of cotton-wood trees, and dividing El Paso from her Mexican sister. A straggling*

*village of low adobe huts and hideously ugly frame buildings, a blot
even upon that dreary landscape.*[8]

Campbell was equally dismayed to find out that George was not her only
bedmate:

*One long street, leading from the depot straight out to the only hotel—
a street in which you sank ankle deep in sand with every step; a hotel
whose chief claim to distinction, I afterward found, were the strength
and variety of its odors, each more noxious than the others, and the
number, size and liveliness of its fleas . . . I don't want to stretch the
truth, but there were millions, billions, trillions of them.*[9]

Fleas aside, south-of-the-border life was "immediately varied and
adventurous."[10] The couple lived in an opulent private train car, which
followed the construction of the Mexican Central Railroad, an extension of the Atchison, Topeka line that connected El Paso and Chihuahua.
When George Tobey Anthony did not win a second gubernatorial term,
friends in government had softened the blow by giving him a position as
general superintendent of the building of this railway. Besides the hefty
salary taxpayers paid him, G. T. made a fortune from buying stock in
this railroad. Leonel's new husband was a "local agent" for the railroad—
someone who contracted for local freight delivery, supervised ticket sales,
and so on.

In her 1900 *Denver Post* feature story about her time in Mexico,
Campbell wrote of her strange new surroundings, and people the likes of
whom she had never seen before:

*Paso del Norte, the little frontier town opposite El Paso, Texas, was
the headquarters of the Mexican Central, and simply swarmed with
thousands of men from all parts of the West who had drifted in there
to work upon the railroad. Low-browed Italians, with their ever-
ready knives; red-shirted Irishmen, with short pipes and a burning
desire for a scrap; meek-faced, hard-working Chinese always huddled
together, their pigtails bristling with fright at the first symptom of*

a row; little chocolate-colored natives, with their big sombreros and
flapping trousers; gold-laced government officials, wearing a hitherto
unheard-of air of importance and an open hand eternally extended
behind them; and, over all, swaying, directing, controlling and slowly
but surely bringing order out of chaos, a handful of energetic, business-
like Americans—the railroad officials.[11]

She also took note of all the hustle and bustle of the center of Paso del
Norte, with endless freight cars, stores, and warehouses. "Huge saloons
abounded" and the "festive dancing hall" ornamented every corner—and
the "evil birds of prey" that hover in every new place seemed to be there in
force: "gamblers, fakirs, and women with vicious eyes and hard mouths."[12]

Soon after the honeymooners arrived in Chihuahua, the senior
Anthony was replaced as supervisor of the Mexican Central Railroad,
but this was not upsetting to the family so much as it was a relief. Father
and son had bought huge tracts of forests in Old Mexico and were happy
to devote all their time to an even more profitable lumber enterprise.
Leonel spent her time doing what wives of wealthy magnates did: she
entertained financiers, government officials, and train executives. "Here,"
says one version of her biography, "her blond beauty was accentuated
by the latest Worth gowns imported from Paris, and the exquisite and
expensive jewels with which George adorned her. At afternoon functions,
her plumed chapeaux brought admiring exclamations from the native
señoras."[13] Moreover, Campbell later wrote, she acquainted herself with
the intricacies of Latin American politics. She was even a guest at the
palace of Mexican president Porfirio Diaz.

Over time, Leonel learned that life in Chihuahua could be pretty good
for those who had the means to enjoy it, as the Anthonys did. Anthony
Sr. explained to one reporter that luscious fruits and roses grew in their
gardens all year round, and the streets were well paved with German and
American investment dollars.[14] Leonel described it as "quaintly picturesque," with great, rambling gardens surrounded by high adobe walls and
green trees. It had "red and blue and brown and pink-decorated houses . . .
narrow streets, jingling carts, herds of funny little burros and crowds of
odd people."

So that her readers would not get the impression that Nell was living a life of luxury in Mexico, she wrote about its dangers, too. "All the other 'bad' towns had had their day when El Paso entered the race," Nell wrote, "and naturally it did its best to beat the record." Tragedies were of daily occurrence, and "shooting scraps were of little or no excitement." She explained that cowboys came in squads off the Texas ranges and, with wild yells or popping pistols, either "took the town" or "got took." When these things happened, the Anthonys "simply hid ourselves to the inside of our rooms, blessed the thick walls, fastened the doors and windows and waited until the flurry was over, when we looked down the one long street." After whatever skirmish was over, she and George or any visitor she happened to have over would take a peek, see two or three motionless forms decorating the unpaved way.[15] When they missed the US, George Jr. and Leonel traveled to Leavenworth, where they kept a home as well.

The marriage fizzled after about four years. News about the couple appeared in gossip columns less and less, and then not at all after 1887 or so. That year, George had gotten a job as a superintendent of the Kansas City West and North West Railroad, and the couple lived in Missouri for a while, closer to Nell's parents. But by 1889, the first Mrs. Anthony had reappeared in society pages, calling herself as such; in 1894, the tables turned when Leonel divorced Anthony, citing "abandonment." Emma Putnam Anthony and George remarried in 1898.[16]

Certainly Leonel did not suddenly pack up one day and quit her position as a society wife to become a cub reporter, pounding the streets of New York City. As is usually true with all relationships, both starting and ending, the couple probably took some transitional time to reflect about whether or not to end their marriage.

But the couple did not take too long, because Leonel was living in New York by the late 1880s. Belford writes that when Campbell left Anthony, she went to New York with a letter of introduction to a friend of her father's, "Colonel" John A. Cockerill, who was then managing editor of Joseph Pulitzer's *New York World* newspaper. The oft-repeated story is that when she interviewed with Cockerill, the formidable copy chief scolded her: "I ought to spank you and send you back to your husband!" This story is all too similar to that of Elizabeth Jane Cochrane, aka

Nellie Bly, who allegedly also walked into the offices of Cockerill, asking for a job.

Cochrane's experience as a fledgling reporter is fairly well documented, because of the contemporary acclaim for her undercover exposé of the notorious asylum conditions on Blackwell's Island. Cochrane received accolades from Cockerill. Leonel wished to have this "origins" tale, too. After all, the story was an ideal one for a Victorian female who wanted to work—she had to have pluck, nerve, and luck. And, she needed a powerful man to bless the fruits of her trickery.

In fact, Campbell did not interview with Cockerill. She may not have worked for the *World* at all. The recent divorcee moved to New York with the intention of becoming an actress—she had long been interested in the dramatic arts and loved the vibrancy and intensity of the city.

She surrounded herself with eclectic and interesting friends, like Dr. Walter M. Fleming, founder of the Shriners; the Platt family, who owned and published the *Poughkeepsie Eagle*; British actor and manager Beerbohm Tree; the Countess de Montaigne, an American-born fashion and society writer; and Thomas Gedney Patten, president of New York and Long Branch Steamboat Company and a future congressman. Campbell performed in workshops for the prolific songwriter and dramatist Emile Andrew Huber and off-Broadway producers. The novelist Alice Howard Hilton nominated her for membership in the American Authors' Guild. And it was here in New York that Campbell made a lifelong friendship with Frances Benson, who would become one of her closest confidantes and a business partner in the newspaper business.

Leonel took a fair amount of jewels, furs, and cash from her marriage to George Anthony, but these were the days before consistent alimony laws, and her funds began to dry up—especially since she lived in costly New York. She decided it was time to get a regular job, and set her songwriting and acting endeavors aside for the time being, though she would come back to them later. According to various sources, Campbell took a staff writer position with the *New York Herald* and then the *New York Journal*, covering events like tenement fires and society items.

Again, this part of her career is probably inflated by later publicity pieces designed to lend her credibility for various endeavors. Articles carrying her byline have yet to be discovered in various newspaper archives, though it is entirely possible she was not given a credit—this omission was common practice with non-feature articles, especially those written by women. For the most part her early journalistic endeavors are memorialized by a highly flattering syndicated newspaper article about her appointment to the St. Louis World's Fair commission in 1903:

> *Mrs. Anthony's newspaper work has been varied in character and in pursuit of her profession she has traveled all over a large portion of the civilized world. Early in her career she was on the staff of the New York Herald and New York Journal, but it was while a writer on the New York World that she first attracted national attention to her work.*[17]

This "national attention" came in the form of those two ruthless Denver businessmen, Harry Heye Tammen and Frederick Gilmer Bonfils.

CHAPTER 2

Colorado, A Cave of Whispers

Leonel traveled from New York to Denver to visit her parents and brothers in the summer of 1898. Nelson and Mary Campbell had relocated to Denver in 1892. At least one son suffered from tuberculosis, and there was no better place to be at that time than Colorado. The state had become known as the "World's Sanatorium," and at the end of the nineteenth century, its curative climate was the biggest driver of its population growth. The young Campbell male soon recovered, thanks to Denver's dry, fresh air and sunshine.

Unfortunately, Nell's brother Alonzo—"Lonzo," as he preferred to be called—did contract tuberculosis some years later, in the winter of 1896. He died that summer, at twenty-two. In addition to her mounting debts, her brother's death may have spurred Campbell to move closer to her bereft parents and siblings.

According to most sources, Campbell met Frederick Gilmer Bonfils, co-owner of the *Denver Evening Post* on a train in 1899. According to Western historian Mary Lou Pence, Campbell was seated across from Bonfils at a dining table and was captivated by his brown-check, braid-edged suit. Then she took a second look and saw he was reading a paper with gaudy red headlines. "How awful!" Campbell blurted out. She was embarrassed when he proudly told her it was his paper, the *Denver Evening Post*. Before the meal was over, wrote Pence, some of Bonfils's enthusiasm had rubbed off on Campbell, and she had accepted a job writing for his "awful" newspaper. For his part, according to many sources, Bonfils was captivated by her wit and charm, and her writing skills, and introduced her to Harry Tammen, the other *Post* owner. The pair had purchased the newspaper when it was known as the *Denver Evening Post* and when it was in dire financial straits, owing to the Depression of 1893 and other misfortunes. Tammen and Bonfils paid $12,500 for it and renamed it *The Denver Evening Post*, though they dropped *Evening* from its masthead in 1901.

Neither had any newspaper experience. Both had plenty of business experience, though not always the most ethical kind.

Harry Heye Tammen was born in 1856, in Baltimore, Maryland, to German parents. His father was a pharmacist by training, though he may also have been an attaché at the Netherlands consulate. The elder Tammen died when Harry was seventeen, and because there would be little money coming in, he dropped out of school and decided to seek his fortune out West. In 1880, after a short stint as a clerk in a print shop in Chicago, Tammen drifted to Denver, which was booming from recent silver discoveries at Leadville, Aspen, and the upper reaches of Clear Creek west of the city.

Tammen found work at the brand-new Windsor Hotel on Larimer Street. He was a combination bellhop, busboy, roustabout, and occasional bartender. According to *Post* historian Bill Hosokawa, the young man wanted to open his own restaurant because "everybody has to eat," but changed his goal when he noticed that almost everyone was interested in mineral specimens, gold-flecked pieces of quartz or just plain chunks of pretty rock. Tourists were flocking to Denver. Why not sell them rock specimens? And so, a year after he arrived in Colorado, Tammen rented a small space at the Windsor and started selling souvenirs—mostly bead-work, furs, polished agates and some turquoise, and curios like "Moon-Eye, the Petrified Indian Maiden," a mummy of some sort acquired from a bankrupt mortician.[1] Tammen purportedly boasted that on a good day, he "could sell the scalp of a single famous Indian chief seven or eight times."[2]

To build his curio business further, Tammen launched a newspaper called *The Great Divide*. It was distributed monthly to those subscribers who paid a few cents for stories about the American frontier, like "Myths of the Iroquois," "Three Indian Chiefs," and "The Cruise of a Prairie Schooner." Sometimes there was a page devoted to the "Women Citizens of Colorado," by suffragette Ellis Meredith. Though Coloradoans enjoyed reading *The Great Divide*, Tammen made no pretense of delivering fine journalism, but rather, his paper was meant to sell both advertising to companies and gem stones and curios to readers. A trade magazine aptly named *Profitable Advertising* extolled the virtues of Tammen's promotional genius, and described a man ready to take the Denver newspaper industry by storm: "Mr. Tammen's features speak for themselves. They plainly show that he is a bright, wide-awake man. He is young as yet in years, and consistency and determination seem to be written in every line of his features. The advertising matter which has appeared from time to time in the different papers comes from his fertile brain."[3]

Through his venture with *The Great Divide*, Tammen became well acquainted with the financial woes of the much larger *Evening Post*, a Democratic paper that had a large subscribership but which was going bankrupt owing to the Depression of 1893 and competition from four other Denver-based papers. Tammen immediately saw the possibilities of growing a dominant regional newspaper—the businessman had watched the city triple in size from roughly 36,000 people when he arrived in 1880, to nearly 107,000 people in 1890, when the *Divide* started turning a tidy profit from its debut the year before. Unfortunately, Tammen did not have the $12,500 cash necessary to purchase the *Post* and turn it into a profit-maker once again.

But Frederick Gilmer Bonfils had plenty of cash. When and where Tammen met this Missourian entrepreneur is obscured by time, but it seems likely that they first met at the World's Columbian Exposition in Chicago in 1893, where so many young men were looking for business opportunities. Bonfils's secretary for the last dozen years of his life, Anne O'Neill Sullivan, recalled asking her boss about the meeting. He told her he won ten thousand dollars in the Louisiana State Lottery and that Tammen read about it in a newspaper and wrote to him, suggesting the prize be invested in a paper that was for sale.[4] There is another version in Gene Fowler's *Timber Line*, a history of the *Denver Post*. In this account, Tammen went to Chicago in 1895 to sell tinted photographs of the World's Fair and then chanced upon the idea of selling copies of the Declaration of Independence. While at the printer, he noticed what appeared to be lottery tickets and learned they were being printed for a gambler in Kansas City named Fred Bonfils. Tammen then went to see the "land shark" Bonfils at the Great Northern Hotel and told this stranger that "he was going to con him out of half a million dollars so they could both make a fortune in a business neither knew much about," and that Bonfils shook his hand, saying with snark that if Tammen got money out of him, he would be the first to do so.[5] Whatever the case, Bonfils had cash reserves from his lotteries, for which he was repeatedly fined for defrauding those who purchased into a pot that no one ever won except friends and family.

Like Tammen, Bonfils moved to Denver to seek new opportunities (and perhaps hide from old customers). It seems the pair were well acquainted by 1895, for their families lived together for a time on Corona Street. The businessmen purchased the failing *Post* on October 28, 1895, and according to a vignette in *Timber Line*, the partners walked arm-in-arm up Curtis Street as Tammen told Bonfils, "It is a piddling little paper now, but we'll wean it on tiger-milk."[6] On November 4, they officially changed the title of the newspaper to *The Denver Evening Post*. In their first editorial, the men promised the people of Denver they could rely on the *Post* to be "fearless and independent . . . the sincerest friend the people have." They promised the best in telegraphic services that would bring subscribers the best and the fastest in news of the world, and this news would be accurate and printed "without fear or favor." The new *Post*, promised Bonfils and Tammen in the first of many slogans the paper used through the years, would be "Not Democrat, Not Republican, Just Independent!" There is, today, a plaque on the sidewalk near the *Denver Post* inscribed with one of Bonfils's favorite sayings: "A dog fight on Champa Street is of more interest to Denverites than a war in Europe!"

"Tam" and "Bon," as citizens came to call them, moved the old offices of the *Evening Post* to a much more prominent address at Sixteenth and Curtis Streets, a corner location across from the Tabor Opera House. As the real estate agent pointed out, hundreds more people would pass by this address than a cheaper one they'd looked at. "'The *Post*' should be where people can see it," he said. Tammen agreed, but added that the people should also be able to *hear* it. The walls of the partners' new private office were painted a flame color. They called it "The Red Room," but it became known to citizens as "The Bucket of Blood," because of its color but also because of the sensational, red-colored headlines the paper would produce.

The city that the *Denver Post* set out to serve in 1895 had only recently grown out of its "frontier buckskin." In the late 1850s, prospectors discovered tiny amounts of gold in this region in the eastern foot of the Rockies, near the confluence of the South Platte River and Cherry Creek. Land speculator General William Larimer named the city after Kansas Territory's governor James W. Denver, in the hopes that this flattery would propel Denver to make it the seat of Arapahoe County and allow Larimer and his cohorts to attract immigrants and their dollars to the community. Unfortunately, Governor Denver resigned his position in November of 1859 and thus had no say about whether the city would become capitol of the territory or not. Regardless, the name stuck, and in 1861, Denver City became Arapahoe's county seat until it became its own county in 1902. In 1867, Denver City became the territorial capital and shortened its name to simply "Denver." Colorado was admitted as a state of the Union in 1876, and in 1881, citizens voted to make Denver its permanent capital.

The decades of boom mining between 1859 and 1890 made millionaires out of those who had had the courage and the capital to develop mineral lodes. Many more became rich from supplying mining towns with food and clothing. Others amassed fortunes from cattle ranching and land speculation. And for those who did not have the capital or wherewithal to "get in early" on Denver's mining boom, there were plenty of government jobs created to support the growth of the city—one could make a very respectable and comfortable living as a clerk, a commissioner, or a law officer of some sort.

When Leonel's parents moved to Denver, Nelson soon found work as head carpenter for the many civic buildings springing up in the city. Roy, Charles, and Alonzo worked their way up from wrappers to clerks and then salesmen at Golden Eagle Dry Goods. Charles became president of the local Retail Clerks union and fought to let clerks of the city organize: "Hon. Charles W. Campbell of Denver addressed the delegates. He had injured his health standing behind counters before coming to Colorado, and knew that the objects of the union were just and their demands reasonable."[7]

When she arrived some time in 1898, Leonel moved in with her parents and brothers into a rented house on Sixteenth Street, in what was called the "Highlands" neighborhood, near the city's civic center. From her home, it was a ten-minute walk to the *Post*'s offices at 1019 Sixteenth Street.

The journalist started work in Denver during a pivotal and rapidly changing time in its history. As one historian described it, the city was "firmly in the grip of boodlers, bribe takers, [and] petty politicians, ready to enter the twentieth century stewing in a vat of malodorous municipal and corporate corruption." These conditions were related directly to explosive growth, and such an expanding population needed a widening spectrum of duties and services that the city found impossible to provide. Because it grew in size and wealth so quickly, politicians and business leaders often squandered the city's resources without thought of long-term sustainability or fairness to all of its citizens.[8] Increasing density and housing shortages posed new problems for city administrators. Many residents who had been in Denver for at least a generation or two resented the influx of new residents from other states and countries.

This infusion of new life in Denver and its environs at the end of the nineteenth century reflected all the contrasts of a boom-town atmosphere. Visitors to Denver would see, sprawled haphazardly in all directions, "a city of broad streets and squalid slums; of dives and churches, of *nouveaux riches* and of college men."[9]

These visitors would also, describes historian Roland DeLorme, find public restraint dwindling and noted a sense of freedom from conventional standards of morality. The raw environment and comparative newness of the population severely strained church ties, and newcomers had to make their own choices of faith and conduct.[10] Without the power of moral suasion, continues DeLorme, church leaders tended to object only feebly to violations of conventions. For example: ordinances that banned Sunday sale of liquor and prohibited the presence of minors in the city's many saloons apparently lacked public support. Clergymen were placated by scattered raids; local officials winked at the liquor trade and ignored the fiery speeches of prohibition advocates.[11]

Against this backdrop, Campbell's first articles for the *Post* appeared in August 1898. The paper provided a preface to her first works:

A dashing young woman from New York is staying temporarily in Denver. . . . She likes Denver, but she loves New York. A brief vacation in Denver is not without its attractions; as a place of permanent residence, New York, with its immensity, its diversity, its rare blending of types and nationalities, and that nameless charm which comes from being the heart which centers and sends for the national impulses is beyond compare. At least she thinks so. But she is here temporarily. It occurred to the Post that a series of articles on various local notables, written in her own breezy style might prove both desirable and attractive.

Campbell, said one reporter decades later, quickly fell into lockstep with Tammen and Bonfils's mission to outsell other Denver newspapers and began investigating diligently, turning Colorado into a "cave of whispers." Allegedly, her colleagues at the *New York World* gave her the pen name "Polly Pry" because of her ability to pry information from unlikely sources.[12]

Campbell's first interview subject, Mr. Charles Spalding Thomas, might have described her "breezy" style as something more like "caustic." Some citizens labeled Thomas a "Fusion" candidate, because he had the backing of his own Democratic Party, but also of some Independents, Populists, and even some Republicans. Campbell paid the media-shy candidate a visit and wrote a piece that put every future candidate on notice that he (or she) could be subject to scrutiny by Polly Pry:

"You wished to see me, madame?"
"If you are Mr. Thomas, yes!"
"What is the nature of your business?"

If tones could freeze, the marrow in my bones would have congealed then and there, the voice of the would-be senator was so icily

unfriendly. Fortunately, it was not the first time I had met aspirants
for political preferment in the first flush of their campaigns, and then
I am not naturally timid.

The newly anointed *Post* reporter used physical description to portray
Thomas as villainous, uncouth, and untrustworthy:

The angular Mr. Thomas did not ask me to be seated; he probably forgot
it. This chasing after high places sometimes makes a man forgetful of
the little courtesies, which is a pity, as they cost nothing and are of great
value where properly applied. Mr. Thomas is not a handsome man,
which is another pity. If he ever gets that seat in the upper house and
gives the cartoonish a chance, I feel for him. He is tall, thin, nervous
and irritable, with a harsh voice and cold gray eyes.

Campbell went on to describe his thin, pressed lips, giving readers the
impression he was an amphibian of some sort. "Dear Mr. Thomas," she
pressed, when he would not say for sure whether he was running for governor, "surely you must have something to say to the *Post!*" "I have absolutely nothing to say to any of the papers," he replied, "and as I am very
busy I must ask you to excuse me." Nell remarked that he did not look
busy, but that he may have wanted to think, and with some men, thinking
required time.[13]

Campbell wasted no time barging into the offices of other Denver
leaders. "I would like to see the mayor!" she demanded of a perturbed
young man guarding the office of Thomas McMurray, who had presided
over the city since 1895. The secretary assumed Campbell was peddling
razor blades or dictionaries and softened his demeanor when he realized
she was there on business. She pressed McMurray, Denver's first bipar-
tisan mayor, on his thoughts about creating a new water utilities plan for
the city, to replace the inconsistent and expensive Denver Union Water
Company. She thought him "a very good looking man," and by the end
of her meeting thought she might cast her very first vote for him, though
she suspected that "he may not be as frank as he looks, and that his
ambitions are probably more powerful than his scruples." More important

than Campbell's analysis of the mayor was her candid assessment of how she was treated as a woman trying to do her job as a professional: "It was a cold shock, being taken for a razor peddler, but I waited while a long string of men who were also waiting went one by one into the room beyond—remained a few minutes and passed briskly out. I got the impression some way that the man in that quiet inner room knew how to conduct his business with mighty little waste of energy, and when it came my turn and I saw the man I was sure of it."[14] Campbell made these frank assessments her trademark.

If anyone thought Nell would temper her writing as she churned out columns nearly daily, they were proved wrong. In fact, her ink tongue became even sharper with those she considered particularly out-of-touch with progressive politics, or hypocritical, or entitled, or perhaps all of these things. For example, she gifted her readers with one exceptionally vicious account of an encounter she had with Reverend Dean Martyn Hart, head of St. John's Episcopal Cathedral in the city. The salacious headline read, "Polly Pry Has a Red-Hot Encounter With Dean Hart." On September 15, 1898, she walked up to his "much neglected yard" and when she approached the door, Hart allegedly bellowed, "Well, what do you want?" Campbell took note of the offensive tone of this "so-called Christian minister," but told readers that she had come up against bullies when working in the slums of New York and, thus, had the courage to stand up to one in Denver.

"What do you want to see me about," demanded the minister.

"I come from the *Post* and with your permission I should like to talk with you for a few moments on several subjects."

"The *Post*! That's nonsense. They sent you here as a joke! Who's [*sic*] the editors of the *Post*?" I enlightened the gentleman, and he broke in:

"Do you want my opinion of your editors?"

"I should be charmed to have it."

"No you wouldn't; you wouldn't print it."

"Oh yes, I would. I give you my word that it shall be printed exactly as you give it."

"Well, I won't give it to you. I know they wouldn't print it and I won't waste my time."

"Well, of course, you know your own language best, and the *Post* is a family paper, but for once I think I can pledge my word that I will give an unexpurgated account of what you say. It may be contrary to law, but—"

At this point, Campbell wrote, the reverend gentleman's face turned crimson, and he yelled at her so loudly that people passing stopped and stared at them: "You're all alike. The papers in this country are indecent. The editors are rascals, the—; but I won't say any more. . . . I have nothing to say; nothing!"

The reporter held her ground. "No British roar yet invented can make an American run," she explained in the published version. She pressed the minister, and he fell right into Campbell's trap, flying into a rage against the press and the people of Colorado in general.

"You have been in Colorado a great many years," she said, "engaged in missionary and church work, you surely have no objections to telling me what you think you have accomplished in that time?"

"The people of Colorado are pigs," Hart responded. "No, I won't say that exactly—the people of Colorado are—the people of Colorado are as much like our Lord Jesus Christ as the Delphian Apollo. There!" And with that, the reverend shut the door in her face.

Campbell printed her assessment of her exchange with Hart, using the coy language that became part of her trademark:

> *He didn't explain exactly what he meant, whether it was that the people were no more like our Lord than they were like Apollo or whether—but it's too big for me. I present it to you as it was given me. That is the very reverend's opinion of the people of Colorado, who for nineteen years have given him support and heaped honors upon him. They are pigs! They are no more like our Lord than the Delphian Apollo!*[15]

Campbell was merciless, indirectly referring to Hart as an "English bully": "The first time he beats his wife he learns to his horror that there are some things forbidden in free America, and no matter how long he remains nor to what an eminence the good nature of our people raise him, he never forgets that first dread lesson and he loathes America and Americanism."[16]

Reverend Hart was an easy target for Campbell—the *Post* even offered an uncharacteristic apology in its paper a few months later, albeit not one from Polly Pry directly. Physically, the minister was awkward, rather hunched, and by the descriptions of his constantly ruddy face, possibly suffered from facial eczema. Although passionately committed to relieving the suffering of the poor and downtrodden in Denver and its surrounding cities, Hart could not fully divest himself of real or perceived snobbishness, having come to America in the mid-1800s with several degrees and a rubber patent, which ultimately made him a fortune in the 1890s. In June 1887, reporting on some Colorado celebrations of Queen Victoria's Jubilee Day, the *Denver Republican* printed some words that Hart later regretted: "If you want to find simplicity of life, perfection of manners, and absolute truth of existence, you will find it in a degree little to be surfeited in the very uppermost circles of English life."[17]

Years later, Campbell would take Reverend Hart to task for denouncing women's suffrage—he blamed it for Denver's divorce and crime rates—but in 1898, she set her sights on a more obvious target for discussion of women's rights: the Mormon Church. Much attention was surrounding one Latter Day Saints member in particular. Brigham Henry Roberts, an elder from Salt Lake City and grandson of Brigham Young, announced his candidacy for Congress in the early autumn, and in November, a section of Utah voted him into office. Roberts was not the first Mormon to win office, but he was the first open polygamist and—perhaps more unpalatable for Campbell—a Democrat. Scores of other reporters across the country discussed whether Roberts should be allowed to take his seat in Congress the following year, since he had taken extra wives before passage of the Edmunds Anti-Polygamy Act, which outlawed plural marriages in the United States in 1882. Campbell, however, decided to widen her scope to the entire existence of the Latter Day Saints. She trekked down to Salt Lake City in September 1899.

"Breezy Polly Pry Tells a Juicy Story of the Mormon Elders," blared the *Post* headline on September 7. Campbell quickly gave her thoughts about the primary newsmaker of that time, congressman-elect Roberts.

She wrote that he was "confident" of his seat in the House, a "victim of a colossal conceit." He was, she said, a man lost in dreams of victories, who honestly believed that he was the instrument with which the Lord would "level prejudices, conquer opposition and ultimately restore polygamy to its pristine glory in this state and force the East not alone to recognize but receive him and as many of his wives as he chooses to travel with." She then took aim at the hierarchy of the Church, especially at President Lorenzo Snow and his two counselors:

> *The first presidency—three slick and sly old gentlemen—Lorenzo Snow, a dotard, who at 86, still dreams of the pleasures of youth and calls himself the elect of God, the chosen prophet of the Lord, who has telephone connections with Heaven and talks familiarly with the seraphim. Lorenzo is a peach. The double-dyed old villain patted my arm, held my hand and told me how he became more holy than other men and how he established that independent phone to Divinity's own private domain.*

Polly Pry complained that she had had to "cool her heels" in Utah, because President Snow required her to submit the questions she would ask ahead of time. "They asked for time to consider them, and that is why I am writing in place of telling you all about it—I am just waiting. In the meantime," she continued, "I am meeting oracles, apostles, elders, saints and the numerous ladies who form their households and are, with a candor refreshing in this day and age, discussing polygamy and other pretty and instructive subjects with a freedom and openness that would make an Eastern man gasp."[18] Campbell went out of her way to laud those who had shown her the beauty and hospitality of Salt Lake City, including some local judges and concierges and newspaper colleagues.

Campbell's criticisms of the Church provided fodder for subsequent articles in the *Post*, which received plenty of mail commending Polly Pry's reporting of it ("Altogether it was very, very funny. We expected before finishing the piece to read that Polly had the temerity to pull Apostle George Q. Cannon galways."). But there were also letters to the editor that complained Pry was leaving key information out of her pieces:

The writer refers to the case of B. H. Roberts, congressman-elect. I happened to be in Utah when he was elected, but I did not vote for Roberts. I do know that he was not elected by the Mormon church, but on the contrary, he being a free silver man, received the majority of his votes from the mining camps, and they are largely non-Mormon. . . . 'Tis true that the Mormons are faithful in proselyting [sic] and made by far more converts last year than any other church. They have become a power and must be recognized as such. Romantic novels, fiction stories and fairy tales are poor weapons now.[19]

In truth, Campbell was not as concerned with Brigham Roberts's morals or right to take his congressional seat as she was with his influence over women's suffrage in Utah. He had been fiercely against women in his state agitating for the right to vote there in March of 1895, when it was convening its first Constitutional Convention in anticipation of becoming a state of the Union. In lengthy debates, Roberts and other opponents expressed fears that if women's suffrage became part of the new constitution, it would not be accepted by Congress. They were wrong—there was enough Mormon and non-Mormon support for women's right to vote to get it in the state constitution with a comfortable margin. But Campbell simply could not allow an avowed anti-female suffrage advocate to reach the lofty halls of the US Congress without taking him to task in the press.

There is no evidence to suggest exactly when Nell Campbell committed herself to women's rights, but her own writing for the *Post* shows that she had expected more from the women in Colorado when she moved from New York City to the Mile High City:

Didn't we have reasons for expecting great things from these, our emancipated sisters?

Imagine, then, my surprise; not a woman on the ticket; not one dear girl recognized!

What's the matter?

That's what I'd like to know. It can't be possible, after screaming all these years for the proud privilege of the ballot, that they are feminine enough to have grown tired of it already. Or has the tyrant

33

[political parties] grown afraid and combined to crush them? Perish the thought! But there is the record—only one or two women in the convention, none on the tickets, and a loss of more than two-thirds the female voters on Capitol hill!

What a tale of defeat! Where is Jane all this time? What has become of all those influential society women who were going to purify the political atmosphere in Denver? Where are the club women who announced their intentions to participate in all the political squabbles and to see that the machines were run honestly and in the cause of morality and good government? Where, in fact, are the women politicians? It isn't possible that the game is too much for them? Go to! I'll never believe it. But if the Colorado women are really "trun down" and suffrage is a failure here, the sex may as well discard all ideas of a pantalooned future . . .[20]

From its beginning in 1895, the *Post* was a supporter of equal rights for women, and in fact, Polly Pry was not the first female employed by Tammen and Bonfils, though she was the first one officially on staff. Winifred Sweet Black, who later married Frederick Bonfils's brother Charles, freelanced for the *Post* beginning in 1897, barely a year before Campbell started working there. Like Polly Pry, Black had spent a few years in New York, honing her writing skills for William Randolph Hearst's news syndicate. She felt the city to be "dreary and dingy" and left after two years, drifting west so she could ultimately get back to her home town of San Francisco, but occasionally submitting stories on a freelance basis to Hearst. She reserved her famous byline "Annie Laurie" for her New York employer; at the *Post* she used her legal name.

There is no record of how the two women got along, but like Campbell, Black wrote strong, expressive opinions. It is even likely that Campbell took some leads from Black with her coverage of Mormonism, polygamy, and suffrage, as Annie Laurie had written articles for Hearst about those topics in 1896. But at the *Post*, as Barbara Belford explains, Black "shelved drama and wit," preferring a style that was a bit more dry and direct than Campbell's. Polly Pry seemed able to fill a need for acerbic humor during Denver's tumultuous years at the turn of the nineteenth century.

"Polly Pry, though she does sometimes stretch the truth somewhat, is worth ten thousand Winifred Blacks," wrote one subscriber, though both women received large amounts of fan mail.[21] By the end of 1899, Black had, for the most part, dropped any coverage of local news and instead supplied the *Post* and scores of other newspapers with fictional sketches and the occasional national news by way of the Hearst syndication outfit. Though leaving her day-to-day appearance at the *Post*'s offices was certainly Black's personal choice, she ceded the ink space just in time, for Nell Campbell was about to break one of the biggest stories of her career.

CHAPTER 3

A Cannibal and Ol' Plug Hat

"Now let's get on with the hanging," directed the executioner. "Release the floor!"

"Wait! Wait!" hollered a beautiful woman on a horse, trotting into the dusty main square of Saguache, Colorado. "This is a stay of execution ordered by the governor," announced Polly Pry, handing the sheriff a piece of paper. Pushing her way up to the platform where Alfred Packer stood with a noose around his neck, Pry told the crowd, "The events that this man is being hung for took place *before* Colorado was made into a state! This," she swept her arms outward, "was all Ute Indian reservation! Packer cannot legally be tried under state law." "Polly," hissed the sheriff, "why are you doing this?" "Because," replied the beautiful woman, "I've learned something, about *helping* people instead of manipulating them."[1]

So goes the end of Trey Parker's and Matt Stone's *Cannibal! The Musical*, a 1993 parody of the events surrounding the life and trials of Alfred Packer, an American prospector who confessed to cannibalism during the winter of 1874.[2] Of course, the film also presents Packer and Pry as becoming romantically involved, among other historical licenses, but it is true that Leonel Campbell Ross Anthony took on the desperate and sad case of Alfred Griner "Alferd" Packer not only to prove she was a heavyweight reporter but also because she truly felt Packer was the victim of egregious brinkmanship by Colorado governor Charles S. Thomas, who had the power to pardon him. Probably no one in the history of the West, however, was convicted for quite the same crime as Packer.

Honorably discharged from the Army during the Civil War due to epilepsy, Packer had wandered around Western mining camps for ten years, doing odd jobs and looking for a solid paycheck. In the winter of 1873–1874, he joined a group of twenty-one prospectors in Provo,

Utah, who intended to cross the San Juan Mountains for gold country near Breckinridge, Colorado. They stopped for rest and provisions at the winter campsite of Ute Chief Ouray located near the present-day Delta, Colorado. Ouray strongly suggested the party stay at his camp until winter had passed, but some of the men got restless, and on February 9, Packer, acting as guide, and five others set out for the Los Piños Indian Agency about nine miles south of Montrose and another safe stop on the way to their final destination. The men were under the impression the trip was about forty miles, and packed just ten days' worth of food. In actuality, the trip was closer to seventy-five miles. Bad weather and rough terrain slowed the trip even more. Just past Lake San Cristobal, the party became snowbound.

What exactly happened while the six men were trapped in their freezing camp has been a subject of speculation since April 16, 1874, when Packer tumbled into the Los Piños camp alone, claiming to have been abandoned by the others. He related his tale of hardship, suffering, and near starvation, yet he looked surprisingly healthy and well fed for a man who had endured such a harrowing ordeal. Packer shunned offers of food, and requested liquor for his first meal. He had some items that belonged to the other five men in his party; he explained this by claiming they had left him behind. He also had money for a new horse and saddle he purchased in the nearby town of Saguache, which was strange because he was virtually penniless when the party left Provo. Agency dwellers—some of whom were part of the original party that had waited out the winter at Ouray's camp—were, naturally, very suspicious. Packer insisted that he had survived the ordeal by eating rosebuds, pine gum, and small game, and that he had borrowed the money from a local blacksmith.

Packer "lived it up" in Saguache for two weeks, drinking and playing cards in a local saloon. Charles Adams, the man in charge of Los Piños, had had enough of Packer's strange behavior, which was supplemented by his already awkward personality and constant epileptic seizures. He talked Packer into coming clean, which prompted the erstwhile guide's first confession of many, which only added to his appearance of guilt. These confessions included various scenarios of natural deaths and cannibalism to stave off hunger. Adams was inclined to believe Packer, and authorized a search for the bodies of the dead prospectors. But he quickly grew frustrated with Alfred, because he claimed he could not find the route he traveled. "You killed these men," said one of the original Utah group, who was assisting Adams, "and you ought to be hung for it!"

Adams interrogated Packer until the latter finally confessed that he and another man, Shannon Bell, had eaten other men in the group after they died of natural causes because of the extreme weather. Packer then said that Bell went insane and tried to kill him, prompting him to shoot Bell in self-defense and eat his corpse. Agent Adams wasn't convinced and accused Packer of killing and robbing the five prospectors. Under pressure, Packer confessed to the killings. Packer was arrested and kept under constant guard in a building on the Saguache County sheriff's ranch. But months passed, and with no bodies found, no evidence of a crime and no specific charges against Packer, the Saguache County authorities weren't thrilled about his indefinite detention at taxpayer expense. Someone slipped Packer a penknife to open the locks on his shackles, and the cannibal disappeared into the night.[3]

Accounts differ, but it is generally accepted that in June of 1874, either a search party or *Harper's Weekly* photographer J. A. Randolph or both stumbled onto the bodies of the five slain men while passing near present day Lake City. There were bullet holes in all of their skulls, and a shanty was found near the spot. Leading from it to the bodies was Packer's well-worn trail, indicating that he had made frequent visits to his victims and had subsisted on their flesh. Nine years later, in 1883, Packer was captured in Dakota Territory, near present-day Douglas, Wyoming. His trial began April 6, 1883, in Lake City, Colorado, at which time he offered up a final explanation of the events that occurred during that fateful expedition of 1873. It reads, in part,

> *I had been acting as a guide for them, but I did not know a mountain from a side of sole leather. When I came back to camp after being gone nearly all day, I found the red-headed man who had been crazy in the morning sitting near the fire roasting a piece of meat which he had cut off the big German butcher Mills.[4] The body was lying far from the fire near the stream, the skull crushed in with a hatchet. The other*

three were lying near the fire; they were cut in the forehead with the hatchet; some had two and some had three cuts. I came within a rod of the fire, and when the man saw me he got up with his hatchet and rushed towards me, and I shot him sideways through the belly. He fell on his face, and his hatchet fell forward. I grabbed it, and hit him on the top of his head. I then lighted a fire and sat up all night. The next morning I tried to follow my tracks on the mountain, but could not, as the snow was too deep. I went back to camp and with sticks and pine boughs made a shelter about three feet high. This was my camp till I came out. I went to the fire and covered my men up and fetched to my camp a piece of meat. I made a new fire, cooked and ate it. I tried to get away every day, but could not; so I lived on the flesh of these men the biggest part of the sixty days I was there.[5]

Packer was convicted of five counts of premeditated murder. The judge handed down his ominous sentence:

Alfred Packer, the judgment of this court is that you be removed from hence to the jail of Hinsdale County and there confined until the 19th day of May, A.D. 1883, and that on said 19th day of May, 1883, you be taken from thence by the sheriff of Hinsdale County to a place of execution prepared for this purpose, at some point within the corporate limits of the town of Lake City, in the said county of Hinsdale, and between the hours of 10 A.M. and 3 P.M. of said day, you, then and there, by said sheriff, be hung by the neck until you are dead, dead, dead, and may God have mercy upon your soul.[6]

The Colorado Supreme Court reversed Packer's sentence in October 1885 because it was based on an ex post facto law. However, on June 8, 1886, Packer was sentenced to forty years at a trial in Gunnison.

Nell Campbell met the notorious cannibal Packer when he had already been in prison for sixteen years. Urged by her bosses Tammen and Bonfils to get an updated story about Packer, but also desiring a change from the streets of Denver during the especially hot and dry May of 1899, the reporter set out for Cañon City by way of the Rio Grande Railroad.

She wrote about her trip using her trademark descriptive language: "Small towns dotted the long line here and there and the muddy Arkansas tumbled in leaping brown waves past us on its long run to the gulf while overhead a fierce sun got in his best licks, aided by his ally, the spring wind and inside the Pullmans we sweltered, admired, and breathed a sigh of relief when the porter announced our station."[7]

Her relief quickly turned to sadness and outrage when she toured the grounds: "For three hours I had trailed after the warden, seen strange, sad things, caught fleeting glimpses of life tragedies and felt the prison atmosphere. Have you ever been in one of those places?" Campbell later wrote that she felt sympathy for the men and women at Cañon City, not only because they usually came from poor circumstances that led them to crime, but because people could come and look at them for twenty-five cents a visit. There were even teen boys, she noted, "the down of adolescence on their rounded cheeks, but brazen effrontery in their glances— young men who had ruined themselves in the very beginning of their lives, middle-aged men with families out there in the world to bear the burden of their disgrace, and old, gray-headed men who, on the threshold of the grave, had staid to commit a crime."[8] Campbell's last shred of any journalistic neutrality splintered away when she was being shown how new locks in the cells worked. She heard a rustling behind her in what she thought was an empty room save for her and an aide, and when she turned around, she caught a glimpse of a "drawn, white face—the face of a boy—a pair of despairing blue eyes," and heard a deep sigh. The sigh stayed with her while she summed her assessment of the prison, but more narrowly, the prison system in Colorado:

> *Five hundred and eighty-eight prisoners! Five hundred and eighty-eight men and women who by their own acts have cut themselves off from their families, their friends, and liberty! Immense number in any place, but when you consider the population of Colorado it is appalling. The last census gave the state only 490,000 inhabitants, and of that number 588 are locked up for crime, another 700 are behind the awful bars of the State Insane asylum, and 1,000 or more in reformatories, jails, country hospitals, poor houses, etc. . . . What is the matter*

with Colorado? Three per cent of the entire population public charges!
Is it any wonder that taxes are high; that public buildings are allowed
to run down; that the appropriations are never big enough; that the
question of refunding her million or more bonds is constantly under
consideration? What is becoming of the wealth of this great, rich state,
and whence comes this huge army of criminals and unfortunates?

It was a question, wrote Campbell, that Colorado would be called upon to answer some day, and her future prosperity would depend on it.

The journalist met Alfred Packer for the first time in the prison's kitchen. She most certainly asked to meet him—the whole country knew where Packer was imprisoned—but she had a story to write, so she used her trademark dramatic flair:

It was the prison bakery, but the men were all out of sight except one
who stood with folded arms before the huge ovens. He was a tall,
broad-shouldered man with glittering eyes and sooty black moustache
and goatee. His hair of the same dead black was parted low down on
one side and brushed forward and then around in a curious circular
way, and his lips curled with a half insolent, wholly sarcastic smile as
he stared cynically at us.

Polly Pry let her readers know that her instincts told her that this particular prisoner was someone they needed to hear more about in the near future:

There was a suggestion of strength, of vital force about the man that
attracted and at the same time repelled, a something that set him apart
from the common herd. Instinctively I felt that those eyes had seen
strange things in their time and that that man had walked to dark
places and gone through the valley of pain.

She asked about his inmate number, which was 1389. The warden replied, "Alfred Packer. Do you want to talk to him?" Yes, she did. Number 1389 was summoned to the warden's office the next day. Campbell noticed that he walked with a "firm tread," and after looking around the room with "a scorching glance," he spoke to her with scorn and bitterness in his eyes. Packer informed Polly Pry that he had nothing to say—that he had never been accurately quoted. "People came," Campbell wrote, "asked for him, offered to help him, talked about what they would do—and went away and wrote reams of slush and packs of lies, and he was tired of it." She described for *Post* readers the awful events of Packer's life and his ordeal in the winter of 1873–1874. And then, she wrote the first of many printed challenges to lawmakers in the state:

> *Colorado, out of her great heart of humanity, has abolished capital punishment and undertaken to make the punishment fit the crime, not as an act of vengeance, but solely as a protection and a warning to her citizens. How, then, can she justify herself for the persecution and detention of this man who has suffered unbelievable hardships and expiated a thousand times over the crime of which he was accused and of which there was no proof! He was given forty years—think of it! For manslaughter—not for murder—he was never accused of murder—forty years! Is it possible that no member of the board of pardons in this great state, from the governor down, has the courage and the humanity to investigate this case and try to right what looks like a monstrous wrong!*[9]

The next day, the *Post* urged its readers to reconsider their previous knowledge of Packer, to consider that heretofore the cannibal had been "held up to the world as an inhuman beast" and "therefore should be safely caged like some wild animal." But the *Post* also urged its readers to set aside thought of the man himself and consider deed and circumstances surrounding the case. "In a state where capital punishment has been abolished and where women devote so much time to humanitarian questions, it seems to us that that Packer case, for the very first time, should be officially considered on its merits and simple justice at last done the man."[10] With the urging of her bosses, Tammen and Bonfils, Campbell decided she would find a way to get Packer released once and for all.

Not everyone was as enthusiastic for Packer's release as Campbell and the owners of the *Post*. Letters flooded into the editorial offices of the newspaper saying that the paper was foolish for promoting the release of a murderer. John Treeble, treasurer of Montrose County, wrote to the paper several times to say he had been at the Packer trial, and the would-be miner was ably defended by counsel, that no one wanted Packer in their group in the first place and that he went along with the prospecting tour simply to rob the other men. "Polly Pry is like many another from the East," Treeble said, "who is led by a sickly sentimentality for the noble red man, or the bad man generally, which they and she calls humanity. She even quotes Warden Hoyt as saying that even if Packer was guilty he has suffered enough. What! For killing five men?"[11] Another gentleman from New Mexico wrote that *Post* readers were being duped by a "sentimental, silly plea for the man-eater." Campbell responded firmly, and pointed out to both men their inconsistencies with the account of Packer's behavior in 1874, and invited them and the public to compare those inconsistencies with the court record.

But just as many Coloradoans wrote to support Polly Pry's efforts to release an aging man from prison, especially since his guilt could never really be determined. "Dear Polly Pry," wrote one, "I beg leave to offer you heartfelt thanks for your noble and valiant defense of Alfred Packer. . . . If he does [go free], it will to a large part be due to your noble efforts."[12] Warden C. P. Hoyt jumped into the fray, supporting Polly Pry's efforts on behalf of his charge: "The man is nearly 60 years of age, and sixteen of them have been spent behind prison walls. He has only a few more years to live, at the most. I believe that justice has been satisfied, and that Packer should be allowed to go out from here without delay."[13]

Campbell managed to get even more prominent office holders to offer their public support. Mayor of Denver Henry V. Thompson, the chiefs of police and firemen, police commissioner and future mayor Robert W. Speer, and many others wrote an endorsement of Campbell's efforts for the *Post*. With the backing of private citizens and nearly fifty prominent civil servants, Campbell challenged the highest elected official in the state of Colorado to do what she felt was right. She published the list of prominent men who had lent their names to Packer's cause, and addressed it to Governor Charles Spaulding Thomas.

On the same missive with all of the endorsements for Packer's release, "Polly Pry" offered a choice invective for one of the most vocal proponents of keeping the cannibal in prison. Otto Mears, the general store owner who testified against Packer at his original murder trial, was still adamant that Packer should remain in jail for the rest of his life. Mears, an entrepreneur who had made and lost fortunes building transportation systems in Colorado, had moved to the East Coast in the mid-1890s but remained influential in the state's political affairs.[14] Campbell gave Mears as the reason the governor would not capitulate, and in doing so, revealed anti-Semitic views at the time:

In fact, he calls himself the "governor-maker" of Colorado. I herewith present him to you: His name is Otto Mears. You all know him. He is a little old man with a shrewd face and a shifty eye, a trader who always has a new scheme and who never gets the worst of a bargain. . . . And the governor is Otto's devoted friend and legal advisor, and he wants to see Otto's picture hung in the Capitol building! It should be done, and under the picture they should print the word: Coward![15]

On October 14, 1899, despite all of her efforts, the board of pardons in Denver did not recommend one for Alfred Packer, voting 4–1 against it. Governor Thomas took the Board's recommendation against Packer's release under advisement, and in December, offered his reason for not offering pardon or even parole: "The story told by Packer in his statement to the board of pardons and in his application for parole is not, in my opinion, the true one. . . . I am firmly convinced that he robbed and murdered his companions, and that the penalty he is now suffering is a milder one than the circumstances justify."[16]

Campbell wrote some bravado-laced statements for the *Post* about keeping pressure on Governor Thomas, but in truth, she might have let the Packer case go as a lost cause, were it not for one little meeting that set off a dramatic chain of events that kept both Polly Pry and Alfred Packer in the public eye for years to come. In early January 1900, a well-known hustler named C. M. Fergen-Bush approached her with an enticing piece of information. He told Nell that an attorney named William

W. Anderson—sometimes referred to as "Plug Hat Anderson" because of his fondness for the wide-brimmed, felt tops—wanted to speak to her about Packer. As it turned out, Fergen-Bush wished to start a tobacco stand, and Packer would be a first-rate attraction if he could be freed. In turn, Anderson told Campbell that he knew a way to get "Packer sprung" and wanted to talk to Tammen and Bonfils about it.[17]

The writer arranged the meeting with her bosses. Anderson explained that Packer's trials had been held in territorial courts although the crime allegedly had been committed on an Indian reservation, which was under federal jurisdiction. He contended that Packer could seek his freedom on this technicality. Bonfils replied that the idea was not new, but that he wanted to confer with the *Post*'s attorneys before authorizing Anderson to begin legal action at the paper's expense. Anderson, Tammen, and Bonfils set up another meeting for the next morning.[18]

Anderson did not keep the appointment. Instead, he took the overnight train to Cañon City, and by all accounts, told Warden Hoyt that he was there to purchase loads of brick for another man in Glenwood Springs, and when they finished haggling over prices, Anderson asked to see Packer. He asked to see the prisoner and according to Hoyt, told Packer that he was there on behalf of the *Post* and that more specifically, Polly Pry had sent him. Somehow, Anderson convinced Packer that he had information that could get him released from prison, and got the prisoner to give him a twenty-five dollar retainer, with the understanding that Packer would pay him more when he received his Civil War pension.[19]

Bonfils, in particular, was furious when he heard this news, and remained so even after Campbell got the naïve Packer to write a revocation of Anderson's power of attorney. He summoned Anderson to the Red Room, and, in the presence of Tammen and Polly Pry, harsh words were exchanged. Tammen accused Anderson of going back on his word and shouted, "You are a cheapskate and a liar and I want nothing more to do with you!" Bonfils added, "They tried to disbar you for swindling a poor widow out of four hundred and twelve dollars, and the *Post* will see to it that you are disbarred for bunkoing Packer out of the twenty-five dollars." Anderson purportedly rose from his chair and said, "I don't allow any man to talk to me that way."[20]

There was a lot of disagreement about what happened next, and many dramatized versions appeared in newspapers nationwide the next day and in the weeks following. But Tammen, Bonfils, and Campbell maintained their version, which was that Bonfils thought Anderson was reaching for a pistol, so he struck the lawyer twice with his fist. Anderson later said that Bonfils leapt at him, grabbed him around the head, and punched him repeatedly. Whatever the case, Polly Pry cried, "Gentlemen, gentlemen. Stop it," and was able to stop the hostilities for the moment. Naturally, Tammen and Bonfils ordered Anderson to leave the building. Bonfils walked Anderson into the hallway; Tammen and Campbell remained in the offices. As they returned to their business, they were startled by two shots sounding from the hallway. "I thought at once that Bonfils had been shot," Tammen said the next day, "I was near the window, twenty-five feet near the door, and I saw Anderson come in, coming directly toward me." What he said next solidified Campbell's heroism for the rest of history:

> *I sunk in a corner near the window, and just as Anderson was about to fire the third shot—being not more than five or six feet away— Polly Pry rushed between us. Bonfils came in a short distance behind Anderson and I think fell or sat down on the lounge. Had it not been for Polly Pry doubtless I would have been killed. By her cool bravery she saved my life. While Anderson was trying to shoot me with her between she presented her own body to his pistol as quickly as he moved his pistol arm to reach me. Others came and soon danger was over.[21]*

Fortunately, for both Tammen and Bonfils, their wounds were not fatal, and quick medical attention prevented either one from getting infection.

Anderson was charged with two counts of "assault with intent to commit murder," one against Tammen and the other against Bonfils. It was decided to try the cases separately. The assault on Tammen went to trial first, in April 1900, three months after the incident. Anderson's attorney chose to plead justifiable self-defense, that Tammen and Bonfils set upon him, intending to inflict great harm. "The first thing he remembered from the shooting," wrote some newspapers, "was Tammen trying to hide behind the skirts of Mrs. L. R. Anthony, 'Polly Pry,' a writer on the *Post* staff."[22] This account was challenged by Tammen, Bonfils, and Campbell.

After another dramatic trial, the jury deadlocked 6 to 6. Following a day and a half of fruitless deliberations, the foreman reported that a decision was impossible. The judge agreed and dismissed the jurors. In July of 1901, fifteen months after the first trial, Anderson was tried a second time for the assault on Tammen. The latter again sung Campbell's praises, offering even more elaboration of how she saved him from the gunman: "Polly Pry then ran between us and yelled to Anderson to desist. He tried to reach over her and shoot a third time. I grabbed her around the waist, and she dodged him, and I did the best I could to get out of the line of the revolver. Finally, I sank to the floor, faint."[23] The defense praised Campbell's reputation as a newspaperwoman, but took issue with her account of shooting. "The story of Mrs. Anthony saving the life of Tammen was grossly erroneous. Anderson had no intention at all of shooting him [Tammen] again," supporting its contention that Anderson shot both Bonfils and Tammen out of self-defense. Defense counsel continued to try to show inconsistencies between Campbell's account of the shooting done just hours after it actually happened, but Polly Pry held her ground, explaining that there would always be small inconsistencies when recalling such an adrenaline-infused event. Campbell's alleged admonishment to Anderson—"Go ahead. And then hang!"—first appeared in Gene Fowler's *Timber Line*, a biography of the *Denver Post*.[24]

Whatever the jury thought of this and the other testimony can't be known, but the result was the same as the first trial: the jury was deadlocked 6 to 6. Anderson went on trial a third time in October 1901, but was quickly acquitted.[25] A month later, Tammen was arrested and convicted for attempting to tamper with six members of the second Anderson jury. He later admitted his guilt, after serving an hour in jail and paying an unknown fine.

As for Alfred Packer: he was finally paroled January 7, 1901, between the first time he'd met lawyer Anderson and the attorney's second trial. His parole was the last official act of Governor Thomas, and Campbell was allowed to bring this paper bearing this news to Packer in Cañon City. Thomas decided to give Packer conditional parole as an act of compassion, noting that the convicted man suffered from hydrocele (water buildup around the groin) and Bright's disease, making his confinement dangerous.[26] Campbell's efforts supported Packer's release as well, even if only when it was politically safe for Thomas to authorize it:

> *He also presents a petition signed by leading men of different sections of the State urging his release under the provisions of the indeterminate sentence act. Without changing my opinion concerning the offense, and because of the second recommendation and additional grounds therefore, I am constrained to grant the application confining the prisoner, nevertheless, within the limit of the State of Colorado.[27]*

Campbell wrote of that cold, winter day made brighter for her and most certainly for Packer, when she brought him his legal release form: "Will you please thank the *Post* and Governor Thomas for me," Packer said with big tears in his "widely dilated eyes," and he tried to thank Polly Pry but he was so overcome with emotion, she wrote, that he could not quite get the words out. She assured him that if he just lived his life in a good manner, it would be all the thanks anyone needed. "It was only 2:00 yesterday that we knew the parole was granted," she wrote, "and at 8:00 that night I took the train for Cañon, where in the middle of the night I told Alfred Packer that his long imprisonment was ended and a new lease of life had been granted him."[28] He spent his last days near Littleton, near Denver, and died from a stroke on April 23, 1907.

CHAPTER 4

Around the World with Polly Pry

Newspapers all over the western United States marveled at Leonel Campbell's tenacious work to get Alfred Packer released from jail. "This enterprising young woman," wrote the *St. Louis Post-Dispatch*, "has now done something which may be looked upon as a triumph. . . . Stern justice may well shiver in her sandals at the outlook. When the young newspaper woman attacks her Jericho, its walls must needs to come down."[1] Two months after Packer's release, Harry Tammen and Frederick Bonfils boasted that the *Post* had three thousand more paid subscribers than its nearest rival, the *Rocky Mountain News*.

Neither Campbell nor Tammen and Bonfils could have known that a year earlier, in 1900, "Plug Hat" Anderson would create such ready-made drama for the *Post* to mine for its readers for the next year and a half. But in between the shooting and courtroom dramas, Polly Pry needed material to write about. She did not waste any time getting back to other matters, covering big and small news alike. There was the new warden at the state penitentiary at Pueblo—a very accomplished man, she wrote, though she felt it only fair to mention to her fellow Coloradoans that he had never held an office—and the directive that women should accept that they are Americans like their husbands and stop trying to separate themselves. About that directive she wrote, "The Woman's club is, according to my horrible opinion, about the most silly fad the women of this country or any other country ever took up." And there were big feature stories, like the one she wrote about Chicago:

It was a terrible proposition that faced the great men of that town, that faces them now. It is the education, the assimilation and the amalgamation of an overwhelming foreign population. Four-fifths of the entire community is either foreign or foreign-born parentage. They are Germans, Irish, Scandinavians, Poles, Bohemians, Italians, Russians and others. They have been pouring in here, day by day, for years, bringing their ignorance, their customs, prejudices, their vices and diseases, to swell the grand total of Chicago's troubles.[2]

One week after the cannibal Packer got his freedom, Campbell arrived in Salt Lake City to cover the National Live Stock Association's convention, at that time one of the most important gatherings in the country. At the end of the month, she wrote a full-page article urging support for Colorado's reinstatement of capital punishment. Yet, she needed a series—an ongoing story that would keep readers breathless until the next installment. She looked to the South and the East.[3]

On May 27, 1900, the *Post* announced that its "vivacious special writer" would sail from New York for Southampton eight days later and take a five-month vacation, during which she would write an exclusive series of weekly articles for the paper. The announcement outlined what readers could expect from their intrepid female reporter:

Her first letter will embrace a story of the trip across the water, which will be followed by one or two letters from London. These letters will be written in her own sprightly style, avoiding the purely conventional and beaten tracks that have few attractions for the general reader and none for Polly Pry. From London she will go to Paris, spending six weeks in that city and at the exposition.[4] An exceedingly brilliant series of letters should come from the French capital. [There will be one or two letters] in which the Paris and Chicago expositions will be contrasted. Few writers are better qualified for such a task, for Mrs. Anthony spent six months at the World's fair as special representative of a New York paper, and during that time saw and wrote about everything of consequence at the exposition.[5]

There is no evidence to show that Leonel Ross Campbell ever covered the World's Fair in Chicago in 1893, and she neglected to mention it even in her more recent 1900 Chicago feature.

But Polly Pry had already proven to her readers that she was up to the challenge of covering other nations and peoples. She had done this regularly in Sunday features since she had arrived at the *Denver Post*, even while her weekday columns were devoted to her coverage of Packer and other progressive and political subjects and, in turn, to the news she made herself while reporting on those subjects. In late 1899, she wrote weekly full-page spreads about Mexico. These stories were about four thousand words, most certainly using notes and remembrances from her time in Chihuahua with George, but perhaps also borrowing from other news services, books, and images culled from the resources of her brain:

BULL FIGHT THAT CAUSED THE BLOOD TO LEAP! POLLY PRY VIVIDLY TELLS THE STORY.

I have seen many spectacles in my life, but for vivid coloring, wild excitement, intense interest, revolting brutality and magnificent nerve, I have never seen that performance upon my mind, and many a night I have awakened trembling with excitement from a vivid dream of that far-away arena, with its glittering sand, its gaily clad men, the crashing roar of the great military band, the deep bellowing of the infuriated bull, the lithe and graceful figure of the famous matador and the suffocating crush of the enormous crowd.

In this piece in particular, Campbell's writing reflected Americans' simultaneous obsession with and hostility toward indigenous peoples. Her description of a "Taramarie" (Tarahumara) Indian who served the then president of Mexico Porfirio Diaz was certainly meant both to titillate her readers and to ascribe an animallike quality to a young man:

I have seen many a handsome man in my lifetime, but never a handsomer nor a more graceful man than the courier who brought in that dispatch. I was present when he was conducted into the presence of the governor, and when he left I gave a long sigh of regret that I was not an artist or a sculptor to reproduce his perfect form and wonderful color. Naked except for a loin cloth; a marvelous red bronze in color; a perfect form, tall, lithe, slender, tiny hands and feet; hair black as a wing; an eye like an eagle, fierce, wild and proud—he could have posed as the "Spirit of the Mountain." He was the one absolutely handsome Indian I ever looked upon.

Just two paragraphs later, in what was surely a reference to the Charlie McComas kidnapping by Apaches in Silver City, New Mexico, in 1883, in which a six-year-old white child was abducted and never found, she wrote:

As the first company swung around the corner, we saw that they carried a long pole, on which a fantastic object bobbed about. As they drew nearer it was whirled about, and the grinning head of an Apache chief was before us. The revolting sight almost took my breath away, but in an instant I remembered that lonely pass near Paso del Norte and the fair-haired boy who had died that awful death, and then I looked with steady eye as each company bore its ghastly trophy past; I looked likewise at the group of Apache women who marched behind each decorated pole.

The Mexican government knows how to make good Indians— they kill them! It's the only way. Late in the week I was taken to the prison to see the captives, and as I stood before a group of squaws, one of them drew from her bosom an ornament of doeskin worked in beads. In the center hung a long, golden curl, the soft and silken curl of a young child, and, holding it up beside my blond hair, she looked with grinning face at the others.

A little child! I could imagine what had been done to it, and I confess that I heard the story of the complete extermination of every male Apache in that band with an unmoved heart—in fact, I saw no reason why those before us should have been spared.

From time to time in the next couple of years, Campbell wrote wistful stories based on the people and places she saw in Mexico in her youth. The "Tragic Story of Conchita, Belle of Nombre De Dios," for example, appeared in an early 1902 edition of the *Post*, littered with "thous" and "thees" among "jefes" and "señors."

And so, with her international reporting credentials firmly established by her coverage of events in Mexico, Nell and bosses Tammen and Bonfils gave Polly Pry's readers some advance notice that she would be developing sources in Europe as well. "Mrs. Leonel Ross Anthony (Polly Pry) has just returned from a trip to New York," wrote the *Post* on a Sunday in March 1901. Never before, it said, had newspapers given fashion much serious attention. Polly Pry planned to interview fashionmongers of Europe at their American agencies and show her readers the latest styles from Paris, London, Vienna, and other capitals. "It will be one of the greatest newspaper achievements of the new century," boasted the daily edition.[6] Two days later, Pry gave her readers a nonspecific preview of what they could expect from the coming fashion season:

The slender, willowy figure is still the model for which all gowns are built. Never before has fat been more fatal to style and grace in dress. High pressure corsets and hot baths, massage and exercise are still required to keep stout women down to the proportions necessary for the proper display of the newest finery, but no one who looks at the result will say that it is not a good thing. Gowns manufactured on both sides of the Atlantic are no fuller at the hips, no shorter at the waist, and no wider at the knee than last year; in fact, if anything, they cling more closely, but thanks be to the gods, it is no longer considered "good form" to have a "wasp-like" waist.[7]

Campbell continued to give her readers fashion news from the European capitals. In September of 1901, after she left London on a "gloomy day, with a cold drizzling rain falling" and took a turbulent trip over the English Channel in which she was tossed about on top of a "dinky little steamer," she arrived in Paris. After shaking off her cold and hunger and getting a good night's sleep, the reporter wrote about life in France's capital:

There were newsboys, the usual type of bright-eyed, impudent little wretches, their saucy faces alive with intelligence, their clothes in rags, but a smile and a jest perpetually on their lips; Jews from the Orient, carrying arm loads of hideous rugs and flaming table covers; white-clad bakers with trays of golden yellow cakes balanced on their heads; pretty girls with baskets of fans and others with trays of flowers; wandering musicians in fantastic costumes . . . tourists; clerks; mounted police. . . . They move a continuous kaleidoscopic, ever-changing stream about the streets, a never-ending picture, a never tiring sight.

She went to the Louvre, the Cathedral of Notre Dame, and the Paris Morgue, where perhaps some of her readers had similarly gone in search of "the horrible, or saddest of sad things, seeking with trembling fear a missing relative or friend, or have even gone into that silent room where under the ceaseless drip of the icy water, covered by the white sheet, the lifeless body mocks at fate."[8]

From Paris, Polly Pry traveled to Berlin, Vienna, Budapest, Moscow, and Saint Petersburg, just like the *Post* promised she would, as she got ready to embark upon her trip in September. "Upon her return from Russia," the *Post's* missive also professed, "she will go to Italy and spend several weeks there with friends. Later, if time warrants, she will visit Constantinople, returning to Denver some time in November."[9] She wrote thousands upon thousands of words about her extraordinary adventures.

In reality, Nell Campbell never set foot outside Colorado. Despite the miles of story she wrote about her travels in Europe, she would not visit that continent for another fifteen years or so. There are no passport applications, ship manifests, or hotel records for any of the names Campbell used at this time. In fact, weeks after she supposedly left the country, she was spotted at a resort in Lyons, a rustic hamlet in Boulder County.[10]

Leonel Campbell was not the first or the last "correspondent" to write fake news stories in the nineteenth and twentieth centuries. There were some reporters on staff at Pulitzer- and Hearst-syndicated papers, the *New York Herald* and the *Chicago Daily News*, among many others, who embellished news stories from overseas wire services or made them up out of whole cloth. These writers were tasked by their employers to serve an American public that increasingly craved news from outside the United States. The Spanish and American War that marked the century's closing years seemed to popularize and proclaim an expansion of America's horizons—an expansion that was already well underway. Shiploads of immigrants arrived in the United States in the late 1800s, totaling almost nine million in the peak year of 1900, bringing people with strange new customs and dress to US cities and stoking citizens' interest in distant places.[11]

Media historian Petra McGillen explains that false news flourished in the nineteenth century, when newspaper and magazine circulation skyrocketed due to cheaper paper and innovations in printing technology. Professional news agencies set up shop in major cities all over the world, while the telegraph enabled messages to be rapidly sent across continents. For newspapers, the problem with these innovations was that dailies started to cover many of the same topics, adopting the same formulaic language and presenting stories in the same formats. Competition in this emerging, fast-paced news business was tough, and with growing standardization, editors needed to figure out how to stand out from the crowd.[12]

One strategy some newspapers used to differentiate themselves from others, says McGillen, was to send foreign correspondents abroad. The idea was that the correspondents could provide stories and analysis from a personal point of view that readers might find more appealing than the "standard, impersonal" reports published by news agencies. However, sending a reporter abroad was expensive, and not every paper could shoulder the cost. Those that couldn't found a creative and much cheaper solution: they hired local writers to pretend they were sending dispatches from abroad.[13]

How did reporters accomplish such a feat, writing—as in the case of Polly Pry—thousands of words weekly about places and people she never even saw? McGillen explains how this was done, using the example of Theodor Fontane, a German pharmacist-turned-journalist who would go on to write some of the most important German Realist novels. In 1860, Fontane, struggling to make ends meet, joined the staff of *Kreuzzeitung*, an ultra-conservative Berlin newspaper. The paper assigned him to cover England, and for a decade, Fontane reported what he "saw," like a devastating London street fire: "I went to the scene today, and it's a terrible sight. One sees the burned buildings like a city in a crater. . . . Fires live on eerily in the deep, and at any moment a new flame can burst forth out of every mound of ash."[14] His readers probably believed him, McGillen writes, because his story confirmed a lot of things they already knew from prior press coverage. Fontane was careful to use familiar imagery, stereotypical descriptions, and well-known facts about London. Meanwhile, he dressed up these familiar elements to make them more entertaining. His own pieces were styled to fit right in with what traveled through the nineteenth-century mass media communications circuit.[15]

All of this is true of Polly Pry, too. A close examination of her "international" work shows very few specifics. It does, however, cleverly play upon prevailing attitudes and prejudices toward people and places:

The museum was what brought me to Antwerp, so it was there that I went first and spent three hours admiring the wonderful collection, which is to Belgium what the Louvre is to France, the very heart of their riches and glory. It is worth a journey from Denver to see the Rembrandts alone. But I am not going to write about the pictures, beyond telling you that I skipped all the martyrs. Of course, it was an awful thing to do, but I'm tired of martyrs, and then I have to anticipate the carnival of horrors I shall be compelled to see in Italy.[16]

Close beside him [Emperor Wilhelm II] rode the Empress Augusta in a habit of white cloth, a skirt that almost touched the ground and a coat that only a German woman would wear. A tiny bonnet of white tulle trimmed with sable tails set well back on her much waved blonde hair, a broad gold band over one shoulder, a belt of the same hue and a profusion of glittering decorations made up a costume that a woman of really refined taste would run from.[17]

Do I like Vienna? Immensely! First, it is a most beautiful city with a host of really magnificent buildings, with a circle of great drives and parks second only to those that make Paris the wonder place of the world, with a bewildering number of grand old churches and public buildings, with a superbly lovely imperial palace and hundreds of stately monuments. . . . Like Paris, Vienna is so gay upon the surface that the underdog quite escapes your notice unless you purposely look for him, but he is here, hordes of him, and no dog in the whole of Europe has a harder time—a more bitter lot.[18]

Sometimes Campbell squeezed into her European pieces her current attitude toward suffrage and women's rights:

I have wished many a time since I came abroad that some of the brass lunged howlers for "female rights" whom I have known could see the practical results of those "rights" as I have. . . . There is no question here about a woman's entering any field of industry. In fact, she doesn't enter; she is thrust into it. They sweep the streets and clean out the stables; they sow and reap and dig and till; they work on railroad tracks, lay ties, build embankments, carry rails, break stone. They build and tear down buildings, young girls, newly married women, women who are about to become mothers, middle-aged mothers of families, and old and decrepit women. They all work at the hardest, roughest, most strength-destroying labor.[19]

Campbell capped off her "European tour" with a visit to Rome, where she got to "watch" the beatification ceremonies led by Pope Leo XIII. She "returned home" in time for the Thirteenth General Assembly of Colorado, which had only Democratic and Silver Republican candidates for the US Senate. She likened the assembly to a "two-ringed circus" and its office-seekers to "ostriches" and "Dodo birds." By luck or by design, Governor Thomas pardoned Alfred Packer a few days later, diverting Polly Pry's attentions.[20]

CHAPTER 5

Tom Horn and Vincent St. John

Leonel Ross Campbell and the rest of Denver awoke to some horrible news on New Year's Day of 1902. Just a mile and a half away from the columnist's home, three young girls and a boy had tired of their Christmas toys and ambled down a ditch to a pool of water that had frozen. The Fridborn siblings promised their mother it was safe, even though it was getting dark. As the children put on their skates, a man suddenly appeared in the trench. He asked if the skating was good, and asked, "Have you got any money?" As the children said "no" and trembled, the man pulled out an ax and ordered them all to lie down. The eldest boy—aged fourteen—knew exactly what the stranger meant to do to his sister and flung himself over her, yelling "Don't you touch my sister." The man killed the boy and assaulted his sixteen-year-old sister. Campbell raced over to the Fridborn home as soon as she heard the police report and then ran to the *Post* to type out a plea to the community:

> *What are you going to do about it? He is here—that unspeakable monstrosity! Here! In the city! He can be found! Are you going to sit down and wait for the police—the police who are doing all they can but who need the assistance of every man in this town because there are not enough of them to cover the whole big city? It is your business! You, each and every one of you, are responsible if he escapes! You cannot evade it—it is your and my and everybody's duty![1]*

The *Post* put up a $1,000 reward for the arrest (by police, detective agency, or citizen) and conviction of the "unspeakable monster" who murdered Harold Fridborn and assaulted his sister. The police department, asserted the *Post*, was "entirely inadequate," and so many tragedies were occurring in Denver that the paper had to provide this financial incentive for citizenry to take matters into its own hands. One reader urged his neighbors to pay heed to Polly Pry's challenge to redouble efforts to find the "brute" and, taking her fervor to a higher level, to turn the $1,000 into $50,000 in order to raise a standing vigilance committee.[2]

No one was convicted of the crime until years later, when a man thought to fit the spurious description given by the children was found living in Canada and tentatively identified. Meanwhile, Polly Pry did some research and told her readers that violence against women needed to stop, that Denver had far too much of it in its history. In "Frightful Record of Assaults upon Women," she implored her readers to do something about rape and domestic abuse, listing the unsolved cases (and names) of thirty-two victims in the prior twelve-month period alone. "What is the matter with the men of Denver?" she asked.

Polly Pry's calls for vengeance merely added to her popularity, particularly among the male set, if letters to the editor and to her personally are any indication. The *Post* received so many questions about Polly's age, and figure, and personal disposition that the editorial staff decided to produce a gimmicky, two-page feature with plenty of photographs and sketches of Pry from its art department, so readers could see how she looked in "real life." Her colleagues from the paper took turns lauding her in this feature, much like signing into a wedding guestbook. The office boy's praise was perhaps the most darling:

> She has been one of the features of the Post since before I was hired, and she will be its great success after I'm fired. She is the daintiest darling of all, and I think her stories are just right. I don't see how she writes them, for all of the times I have seen her she was telephoning to someone else, or joking with someone in the office. If I could ever find a girl who was a good and great woman like Polly Pry I would ask her to be my wife if I had the price.[3]

Of course, Campbell was no girl or even young woman at this point, but at age forty-three, she still looked so youthful that many mistook her for someone ten years younger.

Throughout the first couple of months of 1902, Colorado newspapers ran wire dispatches of sensational events unfolding in its neighboring state. On January 13, just 101 miles straight north of Denver in Cheyenne, Wyoming, sheriff deputies arrested Tom Horn at the Inter Ocean Hotel. The arrest of this stock detective and hired assassin led to perhaps one of the most sensational trials of the year and remains one of history's biggest mysteries insofar as Horn's guilt and what really happened leading up to his incarceration and execution. There was simply no way Polly Pry could avoid inserting herself into this legal showdown, which, even before Horn went to trial, reflected the West's evolution from frontier territory to a place more settled and economically developed.

Horn was arrested for killing fourteen-year-old Willie Nickell, the son of Kels Nickell, a troublemaker and sometime shepherd who had earned the enmity of local cattlemen like John Coble, Horn's employer at the time. At 6:30 on the foggy morning of July 18, 1901, Willie Nickell was brutally killed—shot in the back as he rode his father's horse near the family homestead forty miles northwest of Cheyenne, Wyoming. During the coroner's inquest after the shooting, speculation arose that Willie's killer had actually been gunning for the boy's father. On August 4, 1901, the theory that Kels Nickell had been the intended target gained credence; he was shot and wounded—but not critically—after his sheep trespassed onto a neighboring ranch.[4] After the Nickell murder in July 1901, the county commissioners in Cheyenne hired sometime stock detective and sometime deputy US marshal Joe LeFors to investigate that crime.

In December 1901, LeFors received the first of several letters from a former boss in Montana who spoke of a need for a range detective to investigate rustling in the area. LeFors forwarded the letters to Tom Horn, apparently to induce him to respond.

Horn took the bait and went from John Coble's place in Bosler, where he had been living at the time, to Cheyenne on Saturday, January 11, 1902, where authorities later speculated that he had stayed up all night drinking. He then accompanied LeFors to the US marshal's office the next morning. LeFors hid two people, a stenographer and a witness, behind a locked door. Over the course of a couple of hours, LeFors led Horn into making a series of incriminating remarks about the Nickell killing. The most damaging was, "It was the best shot that I ever made and the dirtiest trick I ever done." The stenographer recorded and transcribed these comments, which were used as key evidence in Horn's trial.[5]

The forty-one-year-old Horn was no stranger to intrigue and violence. At the age of fourteen he left home and wound up in Arizona Territory, then Kansas and New Mexico, working various livestock and stage-driving jobs. While still in his teens, he went to work for Al Sieber, chief of scouts for the US Army, in campaigns against the Apaches. In 1886, Horn escorted the army column that captured the famed Apache leader, Geronimo, for the final time. In 1891, the Pinkerton National Detective Agency hired Horn to pursue bandits who had robbed the Denver and Rio Grande train near Cañon City, Colorado. Over the next decade, Horn did other jobs for the Pinkertons.

Tom Horn came to Wyoming in the late 1880s or early 1890s. He was secretly hired by ranchers Ora Haley, John Coble, Coble's partner Frank Bosler and, probably, the huge Swan Land and Cattle Company.[6] At that time, owners of large herds of cattle were struggling to survive in a business that just a decade before made them extremely wealthy. In the 1880s, they ruled their ranges like "private fiefdoms." Out of greed, they stocked their land with more cattle than the land could support. When a "beef glut" followed by a bad drought in 1886 was followed by a terrible winter in 1886–1887, many ranchers were forced out of business. As immigrant homesteaders moved into Wyoming Territory, the cattlemen who survived began publicly blaming their problems on cattle theft instead of natural market forces. Rustling was certainly a problem, but it was only one of the many difficulties facing ranchers who owned large tracts of land. A few of these cattle barons hired men like Tom Horn to lynch real or alleged cattle thieves to make an example out of them.[7]

The pervasive attitude of Wyoming citizens toward Horn and his big cattlemen supporters was unambiguous. As John W. Davis, author of *The Trial of Tom Horn*, explains, the vast majority of them saw Horn as a "craven assassin" employed by cattlemen who were as guilty as he was. Newspapers openly charged cattlemen with hiring Horn as an assassin, and they opined (or at least hoped) that several cattlemen would be charged with murder as a result of the Horn prosecution.[8]

Wyoming papers might have shown some restraint even when accusing some of its cattlemen citizens of shameful behavior, but some Colorado newspapers—and certainly the *Post*—did not. On March 2, 1902, the daily blared a series of front-page articles by Campbell. One of them was an account of her visit with Tom Horn in jail, where, although he refused to speak to her, she obtained one of the most detailed physical descriptions that exists for him:

> *He is tall, six feet one, but he does not look it, as he walks with a forward stoop, with his head thrust out from his broad shoulders and his chin drooping. His body is extraordinarily long, and although he weighs 190 pounds, he is not fleshy. . . . He has a fine, straight nose, a well-shaped chin, a thin, cruel mouth with a cynical sneer lurking about the corners of his lips.*[9]

"Polly was a skilled writer," writes Davis, "but, more important to the Horn case, she was brash and unafraid to declare some harsh truths." Along with her character sketch of Horn, on March 2, 1902, the *Post* pasted a huge headline on its front page about Wyoming's troubles, which had seemingly come to a head with little Willie Nickell's killing and Horn's arrest: "Wyoming's Appalling Record of Rustler Assassinations Brought to Light of Day." Sprinkled through the page and the rest of the edition were articles written by Polly Pry. Her first target was Wyoming's senator, Francis E. Warren.[10] In her story on "What a Federal Senator Can Do," she blasted Warren as a man who had driven thirty to forty families off public land that he controlled. "And it is this sort of despotism," she concluded, "that has brought about conditions that make it possible for men like Tom Horn to live in a supposedly law-abiding community."[11]

In fact, wrote Pry, Wyoming had a long history of enabling murderous cattle barons. One of her longest pieces was headlined "Long Record of Murder." Davis notes that she had obviously spoken with Wyoming people who had told her of the violent history of the state's cattle barons, though she could just as easily have researched this in older newspapers. She wrote about the 1889 killings of Ellen Watson and James Averell and numerous other assassinations. Pry obtained a copy of Asa Mercer's

1894 book *The Banditti of the Plains (The Crowning Infamy of the Ages)* and presented Mercer's flaming indictment of Wyoming cattlemen for the Johnson County invasion. Pry concluded that by 1892, the big cattlemen "had rolled up a record of fifteen cowardly and brutal murders, and the small farmers throughout the commonwealth were in a state of terror." She concluded with an intrepid declaration of what was at stake in the trial of Tom Horn:

> *If Horn alone were concerned, he would hang tomorrow.*
>
> *But—holding the good name and honor of so many men of wealth and prominence in his blood-stained hands—he still sees a fighting chance for himself.*
>
> *The coming May term of court will determine whether the people of Wyoming will again stand aside and see a few men—who have deliberately appropriated vast tracts of the public domain and enriched themselves at the expense of the state, and who stand for nothing except their own interests—openly defeat the ends of justice and, by the expenditure of their ill-gotten gains, again turn into an unnatural monster loose among the people, or whether the public has now arrived at that point where they will demand that the axe be applied to the very root of the evil and let the chips fall where they may.[12]*

In fact, as Polly Pry's columns suggested, Tom Horn may not have killed Willie Nickell because the Nickells were purported cattle stealers, but Baron John Coble may have used Horn to exact vengeance for rather more personal reasons. A Cheyenne resident gave Polly Pry some background on this rivalry:

> *Coble hates Nickell like the devil hates holy water, and because of that, he wants his land. But he never had an excuse to go after him until Nickell brought in all those sheep. . . . You see, they had a row a good while ago [1890] and Nickell gave him a slash that was a long time healing, and Coble isn't a man to forget. He's vindictive to the last degree and never forgets when he has a score to settle. . . . He drinks a deal and is ugly, overbearing and dangerous when in his cups. He'll*

stick by his friends, but his friends must stick by him in everything, and he always carries the whip hand.[13]

To put an even finer point on things, Campbell wrote, cattlemen as a group were as much opposed to hired assassins as anybody else. Who was to blame, then, if the livestock barons were innocent? It was the residents living in the Iron Mountain neighborhood of the assassinations, she explained, because they refused to hold people like Horn accountable to the law. Davis writes that Pry left the impression that Tom Horn could not expect the backing of a united community of Wyoming cattle barons. He was largely on his own before the bar of justice.[14]

In October 1902, when evidence was still being heard in Horn's trial, Polly Pry wrote a provocative article titled, "When Is 5 Cents Worth $12,000?" She spoke of the facts that Horn, when arrested, had only had five cents to his name, but that within three days, $12,000 had been forwarded by John Coble and possibly some other cattlemen, for the payment of talented lawyers to defend him. Pry asked rhetorically: "Why is the protection of Tom Horn worth $12,000 to Mr. Coble and his associates?" "What crime have these wealthy gentlemen committed, aided or abetted, of which Horn is cognizant, that they should seek, not alone by their money but by their all-pervading influence, to defeat the ends of justice and to again turn an unnatural and terrible monster loose among their people?" She concluded that these men were only trying to protect themselves and that they should be prosecuted as vigorously as Tom Horn had been. Campbell declared, "The conviction of Tom Horn should be followed by the arrest, the prosecution, the conviction, and the punishment of the men who instigated his crimes."[15] A prominent defense attorney from Casper wrote Campbell to tell her that her story "struck the nail right on the head." His own client, notorious fugitive Charles Woodard, who fatally shot a sheriff, was lynched by a mob before his case could be appealed. Woodard "had no wealthy backers," he said, and was hung without due legal process. "This man [Horn] will go free."[16]

Tom Horn did not go free. He was convicted on October 23, 1902, in a Cheyenne courtroom and sentenced to hang; his sentence was carried through a little more than a year later. To no one's surprise, writes Horn biographer Larry D. Ball, Polly Pry strongly approved the conviction, saying: "Wyoming has awakened. She has put out her fair hand upon the plague spot in her domain—and more, she has spoken in no uncertain voice—the spot must be removed. There are to be no more licensed killers in her beautiful kingdom. No more children are to be murdered for the gratification of any man's vengeance—if she can help it."[17] Ball notes that the *Wyoming Derrick* concurred with Polly Pry, carrying several of her stories on its front pages after Horn was convicted. Pry's articles carried weight in Wyoming public opinion, says Ball, because the *Post* was following not leading Wyoming public opinion, expressing thoughts to which Pry had been led by Wyoming people.[18]

While Campbell might have been safely following public sentiment about Tom Horn, she took some bigger editorial risks with events that were unfolding right about the time that Tom Horn was on trial. These events also circled around an assassination. On the night of November 19, 1901, Arthur Lancelot Collins, the young English manager of the Smuggler-Union Mine, a significant silver supplier in Telluride, Colorado, was shot while playing bridge with his friends. He screamed, "I'm shot!" and collapsed, his bleeding body sprawled over the card table.[19] Despite the tireless work of surgeons and nurses, three of whom worked for Telluride's Local 63 union, which was affiliated with the Western Federation of Miners (WFM), he died the next morning. A week later, a judge issued an order authorizing the county sheriff to subpoena a special grand jury to investigate the killing.

It turned out that Collins had no shortage of enemies, owing to his temper and his business practices. He was an outspoken racist, claiming English, American, and Swedish miners were superior to Italians, Austrians, and Finns. He had a particular, public hatred for Italians, hiring them only at incredibly low wages. Collins was notorious for what the *Ouray Plaindealer* called his "somewhat dictatorial . . . manner" and his "mulish disposition." His domineering attitude made him many enemies among the miners, nonunion and union alike.[20] But the miner's union, Local 63, clearly had the most collective animosity toward Collins, and this union group was led by a charismatic young man named Vincent St. John.

Nicknamed "The Saint," St. John was born to parents of Irish-Dutch background in 1876. During the next fifteen years, his family moved around frequently, residing in four different states before finally settling in Colorado in 1895, when St. John was nineteen years old. In Colorado he began working as a miner and union organizer. Within five years, at the age of twenty-four, he was elected president of his WFM local in Telluride. The next year, the Telluride local was involved in a hotly contested strike. One of the mine owners organized an anti-union "Citizen's Alliance" to oppose the striking miners. Scabs were armed and deputized by the police. In response, St. John ordered 250 rifles and fifty thousand rounds of ammunition for the union. As the strike dragged on, a confrontation between scabs and strikers occurred; shots were fired and a few men killed. At the end of the battle, the scabs withdrew, and the strikers occupied the mines. It was about a year after this strike ended that Collins was killed.[21] Little evidence existed to implicate St. John, but Polly Pry was determined to pin him to the crime. Campbell was both anti-union and anti-Irish, which made St. John a natural target for her. Her sentiments probably derived from both personal and environmental experience. A staunch Scots Presbyterian, she held the same anti-Catholic disposition as many other Protestant faithful. As a Coloradoan, she held the same anti-Irish dispositions as many who had lived there for generations, owing to the flood of immigrants to Leadville in the 1870s and 1880s who labored on the cheap in the silver mines there. A generation later, these immigrants settled thickly in Denver, where they played a large role in civic affairs and building the city. As is true with most times in American history when one group of people seems to be taking jobs from others, prejudice followed. Campbell could be especially vitriolic in her writing about people of Irish descent.

The columnist sent a message to St. John soon after Collins's death asking if he would see her, and he acquiesced. Campbell rode out to the Smuggler mills in Telluride early Monday morning, November 24. Someone showed her the chair and the perforated window, "mute evidence" of the crime, and then she toured each floor of the big stamp mill until she reached the top, where she looked out at the "white desolation" of the mountain. She linked labor unrest in Telluride with the unrest that had occurred decades earlier in Pennsylvania, where secret Irish society members called Molly Maguires committed violent assaults and murders in response to miserable working conditions:

> *Law-abiding citizens are startled with anonymous letters, marked with deathshead and dagger, ordering them to leave their homes and businesses or accept the death that is decreed them. One mysterious disappearance after another has startled the community, and now the deadly assassin has started upon his rounds, while the whole community waits with shrinking hearts for news of the next blow.*[22]

Still "trembling with the memory of that cowardly murder," Pry knocked on the union headquarters of St. John, the man "openly accused of being the firebrand who has turned the hitherto peaceful camp of Telluride into a place of terror," and peppered him with questions about the murder:

> *"I wish you would explain to me the causes that led up to the deplorable crime of last week," she asked.*
> *"So far as I know, there was no cause," replied St. John.*
> *"Was there any friction between Mr. Collins and the union just prior to his assassination?"*
> *"No, not any more than there always was . . . but the union had nothing to do with that affair."*[23]

Pry assured him that no one thought that the union as a whole would do something like kill Collins but returned to the question of whether a *miner* might have done so on his own volition. "Who else would have any reason to seek his life?" she asked. "I don't know anything about it," St. John said, "but he had plenty of enemies." St. John's response was bolded in the *Post* article: "Not any more than he made himself. . . . If a man decreases the earning power of his men, he is liable to make himself objectionable." The *Post* readers could not miss the importance of this emphasized passage. Campbell then asked St. John some loaded questions about how much money he made as the head of a union rather than a day laborer—questions that he answered honestly. His answers did not prove a point for Polly Pry; he made quite a bit less than his expenses.

Campbell may have felt she was not getting very far in proving St. John a man who took advantage of union labor. Her next series of questions and his purported answers caused an uproar in the newspaper and mining communities. She asked when St. John thought the owners of the Smuggler's mine would open it up again, and if they did not, what effect that would have on the union and the community at large. "The Smuggler won't close down," he said. "They are just bluffing. I'll eat my hat if they don't open up inside of a week. . . . No matter what they are doing, it's only a bluff—they'll open up all right, and there won't be any other mine closing up either." Campbell said, probably coyly, "You seem to be very positive in your statements." St. John's response—as recorded by Campbell—was also bolded: "Yes, I am, because I know. The whole truth is that there is no trouble with the miners; it is the citizens of this town. There are two or three people in this place that ought to be removed, and then we'd get along all right." Campbell asked if St. John would tell her the names of those two or three citizens of Telluride; he did. One was Charles Painter, owner of the *Telluride Journal*, and the other was Addison M. Wrench, founder and president of Telluride's First National Bank.

The insinuation was clear . . . and explosive. Painter and Wrench were openly anti-union, and Polly Pry's statement made St. John appear to be goading union members to assassinate them. In addition to this, Pry asked the union leader what he thought about all the "mysterious disappearances" around the camp in the prior year, a loaded question meant to imply that organized labor had murdered many enemies— though no instances of this were ever proven true.

The *Telluride Journal* and its city's merchants and mine owners showed restraint when refuting Polly Pry's story, at least initially. But they did spell out specific details that seemed to douse any incendiary flames from Pry's labeling of St. John as a "firebrand": "St. John arrived in Denver yesterday morning and in this morning's *News* has an interview in which he denies Polly's statement, and says, 'I never advocated the removal of anyone at Telluride,' and added further that the notoriety that has been given the disappearance of [disaffected union workers] Barney and Smith is due to a certain clique in Telluride." In other words, St. John denied he had ever advocated for violence in or around the mines.[24]

Campbell stood by her story, putting a rebuttal in the *Post* the day after her interview printed—no doubt she and her bosses had received angry telegrams from the *Telluride Journal* and other area papers the prior evening. She wrote, "In answer to Mr. St. John I have only to say that the interview took place exactly as described by me, and that every word printed in the *Post* and signed by myself is the exact and absolute truth. . . . I have interviewed a majority of the public men of Colorado on a wide range of subjects, and I think that any one of them will testify to the fact that I never deal either in untruths or exaggerations when it comes to the quotation of a statement." She offered up her detailed notes to whomever wished to examine them. Moreover, Campbell said, the *Post* offered to give St. John and the federation the opportunity, if they desired, to respond to any story written by Pry. According to her, both the WFM secretary treasurer William D. Haywood and St. John told the *Post* that they declined this offer . . . only, they then decided to give a statement to the *Post*'s rival, the *Rocky Mountain News*: "You may say for me," said St. John, by way of the *News*, "that I never made the incendiary statements attributed to me by one of your evening contemporaries regarding the 'removal' of several men at Telluride. We are not anarchists up there and the members of the miners' union are law-abiding people."[25] The *San Miguel Examiner* denounced Campbell even more strongly:

> *After lauding St. John on his sagacity and intelligence she must think readers are a pack of idiots to believe St. John made any such incendiary statements as were credited to him. He would have been a fool had he done so, and no one credits him with being anything of that sort. Plain fact of the matter is—Polly Pry lied.*[26]

Polly Pry's employers showed their support for her—at least initially—by printing a "Note by the Editor" underneath her claim of truthful transcription of St. John's remarks: "During the long career of Polly Pry as a writer the veracity of an interview by her has never before been questioned."[27] The furor over Campbell's perhaps truthful, perhaps slanderous interview of Vincent St. John did not preclude the *Post* from printing more stories from her time spent touring the Telluride mining camp. She interviewed one O. B. Kemp, chief clerk of the Smuggler-Union mine, quizzing him at the scene of Collins's shooting:

"Where do you think the person who fired the shot stood?" Mr. Kemp took a pencil from his pocket and kneeling down before the window placed the pencil in one of the round holes with which the glass was pierced and said: "If you look through this hole you can tell about where the assassin stood; this seems to have been the central shot." And I knelt down and looked out to where a brown stump stood, just in the shadow of a dark pine tree, above which the electric light tower reared its red arms. "I should think that the gun rested on the top of that stump, or else the murderer stood just before it," I said, and Mr. Kemp replied: "Yes, that is our opinion also."[28]

It was also Mr. Kemp's opinion that trouble in the Smuggler-Union mine, including all the strikes, accidents and money troubles, stemmed from unionization. He showed Campbell the bunkhouses and foodstuffs set up for the workers but lamented that "a single glimpse of the manner in which the men used them would be enough to convince anyone that the existing conditions were mostly the men's own fault."[29]

But as the days and weeks wore on, Tammen and Bonfils received mounting complaints from organized labor, reminding them of the *Post*'s previous support (or at least benign neglect) of the WFM. The gentlemen sitting in the "Bucket of Blood" office probably would have considered this just a passing nuisance were it not for St. John's announcement of a boycott against their newspaper. On December 7, 1902, the Western Federation of Miners chapter in Telluride, led by Vincent St. John, announced a boycott of the *Denver Post* because of the allegedly slanderous remarks by Campbell. This strike soon spread to other chapters, including the Ouray Miners' union in San Juan County and the Cripple Creek one in Teller County.

On December 12, 1902, a small article appeared in the *Denver Post*. "'Polly Pry' Is Missing," it said, and offered a one hundred dollar award for news of her. "There is a good deal of suppressed excitement in the air just now, though verbal expression of it is carefully guarded," the piece continued. "It relates to the mysterious disappearance of Polly Pry. The matter has not been made more public through fear that some harm might come to the missing one." Clearly, this advertorial was tongue-in-cheek, acknowledging that Campbell had stopped writing until the *Post* stood its ground and stood behind her with regard to the boycott or perhaps that she was simply taking some time off until the furor died down.

Campbell eventually came back to work, writing a sentimental feature about the Christmas spirit and those who gave to charity all year round. She wrote up a laudatory interview with steel magnate Steve Moffat, who was bringing more jobs to Denver, and profiled her friend Senator Edward Wolcott, who was about to make an unsuccessful bid for reelection. She called so much attention to a scheme by a Cañon City penitentiary to publish a "yearbook" of inmates that Governor James Peabody forced its board of commissioners to cancel the project.

But the union boycott of the *Post* did not cease and seemed to be gaining even more participants every day. On February 21, 1903, Bonfils had his paper print a letter from "Big Bill" Haywood, at that time still secretary treasurer of the WFM. It was addressed to Tammen and Bonfils and read,

> *Gentlemen—Numerous inquiries are being received at this office relative to the attitude of the Denver Post toward organized labor. Those inquiring believe the Post to be unfair owing to an article which it published on Thursday, Nov. 27, 1902, assailing President St. John of the Telluride Miners' union. In as much as you have fully acquainted yourself with all of the facts and circumstances leading up to and influencing the writing of that article, I have no doubt but what you are thoroughly convinced that a great injustice was done Mr. St. John directly and to the union indirectly. Believing that the Post is ready and anxious to render justice to every man, however exalted or however humble his station in life may be, I suggest that if the Post were to publish a statement of its attitude in this matter it would advise the*

laboring people of the state of its friendliness and fairness and also do justice to those who have been injured by the article in question. Yours very respectfully,
   Wm. Haywood

The *Post* printed a long-winded reply, underneath its trademark headline, "So the People May Know":

My Dear Sir—In reply to your letter of February 16th, the Post is very glad to take up this matter in order that the harmony and good feeling that has always existed between it and organized labor in the West may not be broken and that there shall be no permanent misunderstanding between us. . . . The Post has tried, and honestly tried, always to be right, but as all human agencies are uncertain and sometimes wrong, so is the Post, but whenever it has been shown that a mistake has been made, or an injustice has been done, we have always hastened to make such honorable amends as were in our power. The Post has always fought day in and day out the battles of labor, and for but one reason, namely, because we believed in the absolute righteousness of the cause of labor.

After another paragraph consisting of effusive compliments toward labor and claims of neutrality in its reporting, the *Post* circled about as closely to an apology as the newspaper had ever gotten:

Now then, taking up the article published in the Post on Thursday, November 27th, in relation to St. John . . . Our correspondent, Mrs. Anthony, or "Polly Pry," was sent to Telluride with but one instruction, which was to get all the news of the situation without fear or favor. The Telluride citizens were at that time in a frame of mind bordering upon frenzy. The mine operators stood almost paralyzed at the assassination of Mr. Collins. Information and news was colored by the sources from which it came, and in the spirit of absolute fairness the Post desires to state that it published statements concerning St. John, which neither his conduct before nor since has warranted. . . . We could have no malice against him, and certainly he is entitled to and will receive at the hands of this paper every consideration that justice and fair play demand.

F. G. Bonfils[30]

On February 23, 1903, union miners, their families, and members of related unions called off their boycott of the newspaper. The newsboys and truck drivers that delivered the paper to neighboring counties and towns returned to their jobs for the *Denver Post*. Leonel Ross Campbell did not.

CHAPTER 6

Parting Ways with the *Post*

In the spring of 1903, news writer Frank Lundy Webster wrote a series of explosive exposés about the Fort Lewis Indian School. Located in Durango, about 340 miles from Denver, Fort Lewis was decommissioned as a military fort in September 1891 owing to the relative peace between Utes, Navajos, and white settlers. The land and the buildings were transferred to the Department of Indian Education to be used as an Indian boarding school. When Webster's pieces ran, this boarding school for Native American children had been in existence for ten years.

"Better might the Indian father abandon his child on the sands of the cactus plains," wrote Webster, "trusting that it might be suckled at the dugs of a she-wolf or be torn by the fangs of a horde of coyotes, than let it grow up to be educated at the Fort Lewis Indian school, if the stories of shame and lust which have been told to me by former pupils and employees during the past two days are true."[1] They were true. Eventually, because of the *Post*'s investigative journalism, Colonel Arthur M. Tinker, inspector of Indian schools for the US government, traveled to Colorado from Massachusetts and upon performing his own investigation found that the school's headmaster had been routinely molesting the female students at the school for years.

But it was Leonel Campbell who originally broke the story. Webster acknowledged that she had been the one to expose the wrongdoings a month before him: "Shocking as were the facts made public by Polly Pry, they prove to be only hints at the awful truth, in light of subsequent disclosures."[2] In fact, Campbell's multipage feature about the wrongdoings at Fort Lewis was one of her most heartfelt, detailed and deeply researched pieces. The *Post* staff knew only rumors about the school; Campbell herself had received a tip from a laundress at the school and decided to go see if she could find out the source of those rumors because she believed that "every man and woman and every little child, no matter what its race or color, or how poor or friendless its estate, is entitled to the fullest protection afforded by our laws and government." With this objective in mind, she booked lodgings in Durango for a ten-day trip.

Once at Fort Lewis, Campbell located and spoke to many men and women and girls associated with the school and gathered heartbreaking testimony of sexual abuse, child labor, and filthy conditions, allowed and usually perpetrated by the superintendent of the school, Dr. Thomas Breen. "I don't know how [all of] this strikes you, my friends," Polly Pry wrote, "but it seems to me the government owes these little ones something better."[3] And, in fact, Frank Webster eventually found that Colonel Tinker's reports did not go far enough in exposing the severity of the problems at Fort Lewis: "The extent of the testimony he has thus far taken is not made public," wrote Webster, "but in the cases in which he has known to have investigated he has acted like an attorney for the defense, accepting as little of the voluntary testimony as possible and objecting to its admission wherever an excuse is possible."[4] In July of 1903, Special Indian Agent Charles S. McNichols found Superintendent Breen guilty of "drunkenness and inefficiency, immoral conduct . . . not only with the Indian pupils, but also with the teachers, and the debauching of Indian girls and sending them to their homes pregnant." Breen was removed from his post. William Jones, commissioner of Indian affairs in Washington, DC, said that the *Post* had engaged in "grossly sensational newspaper attacks" against Fort Lewis but that "the fact remains that the gravamen of the *Post*'s charges is admitted."[5]

Polly Pry was not in the offices of the *Post* when word came in July that Breen had been removed. There are no extant notes about Campbell's departure from the newspaper that had given her a new life in Colorado, but given Bonfils's apology to St. John and Webster's acquisition of her story about Fort Lewis, it seems likely that Campbell and her bosses parted ways. "It was simply good business," writes Barbara Belford, "to offer up Polly as reparation [to St. John], so Bonfils and Tammen refused to stand behind her."[6] In early 1904, labor reformer William English Walling traveled to Denver to study labor issues there and summed the *Post*'s situation with regard to the St. John affair: "The Federation is unquestionably militant. The *Denver Post* published an article two years ago derogatory to the president of the Telluride union. In three days the paper lost 1,500 subscribers. The writer of the article was discharged."[7]

Campbell, Tammen, and Bonfils parted on friendly enough terms. Later, when mining concerns raised their ugly heads again, Campbell put a disclaimer in one of her *Polly Pry* issues in which she explained her position with regard to Vincent St. John:

> *For these [anti-union] statements . . . Messrs. Haywood, Coates, Sullivan and Moyer eventually succeeded in convincing Mr. Bonfils that it was to his business interest to make some sort of reparation to Mr. St. John. . . . For that "reparation" I have no criticism or comment, as I believe that every man has a right to run his own business to suit himself. Of course it terminated my connection with the Post, but it did not alter my loyalty towards a concern that had given me a living for four years, nor did a difference of judgment and opinion change my feelings towards two men who had been for that length of time not only my employers but my friends.[8]*

On April 12, 1903, the *Post* made a grand announcement about Polly Pry's new endeavor: Governor James Peabody designated her one of seven commissioners to represent Colorado at the 1904 World's Fair in St. Louis. Notably, she was the first and only female to be appointed to the commission, and the article was accompanied by a beautiful, youthful photograph of Campbell dressed in an off-the-shoulder gown, tapered at her slim waist with rosebuds adorning her décolletage. The grand article acknowledged her contributions to the paper and to Denver at large (though it also subtly took credit for her success):

> *So favorably an impression did "Polly Pry" make on the readers of the Post that she was prevailed upon to remain in Denver as a regular member of the Post staff. Since her connection with the Post her work has become well known, and she is today conceded the brightest newspaper woman in the West. She has a gift few possess; of writing*

equally well on any subject. Her range of topics is extreme, and yet,
no matter how at variance they may be, the work is uniform, concise,
plain, forceful.[9]

The fair, known formally as the Louisiana Purchase Exposition, was to be held in St. Louis from April 30 to December 1, 1904. Millions of people from across the globe would converge over these seven months to experience the latest achievements in technology, fine arts, manufacturing, science, civics, foreign policy, and education. Forty-three out of the forty-five states of the union would provide extravagant exhibits, showing off the unique business, agricultural and cultural aspects of their states. To be a commissioner for one's state was a huge deal—commissioners had significant financial responsibilities and were expected to make sure every dime spent on promoting their state earned a return on investment in that state in the years afterward.

That Campbell was the first female appointed to the commission was somewhat overshadowed by the way in which she was nominated. Two months before the announcement of her appointment, in February 1903, Polly Pry published a piece that asked for an increase in budget for the Fair Commission from $50,000 to $200,000. She explained that the original amount, appropriated by the office of Democratic governor James Orman, was "ridiculously inadequate" considering the "magniture" of the state. She summed all the clerical and travel expenses that would be required of a proper exhibition at the fair and reminded her readers that Colorado was embarking on an era of prosperity like no other state:

Thousands of men are already at work opening a highway into a
new and marvelously rich territory. Other workmen are breaking
the ground for an industry which should provide employment for
thousands of toilers. The whole state is teeming with promise and
smiling with the fullness of her riches. It is predicted that the city of
Denver is on the eve of an era of growth which will double her pop-
ulation in the next two years. Prosperity is smiling at you—all you
have to do is take her by the hand and show the world the beauty and

glory of her. The great Louisiana Purchase exposition is your opportunity. It's up to the legislature to utilize it.[10]

Ultimately, the Colorado legislature allocated $100,000 for the fair, but this was not just because of Campbell's pleadings. The *Chicago Inter Ocean* broke the behind-the-scenes story and told how Polly Pry's appointment really came about. In an article entitled "What It Costs to Name the 'Colorado,'" the paper described "the climax of an interesting social war that has involved a US Senator, a Governor, a millionaire, two interesting young women, and incidentally tied up an appropriation for a world's fair exhibit."[11] In this "tangle," said the Chicago paper, was also the question of selecting a woman member of the world's fair commission for Colorado—the only woman to serve on such a board. For although females had historically served on separate women's boards, it had never been customary to appoint a woman member to a place on the "commission proper"—in any state.

The chain of events leading to Campbell's appointment started with a ship named the *Colorado*. Due to be completed in January of 1904, this cruiser would be the largest the US Navy had yet built. It was customary for the wife or daughter of a dignitary from the state after which these ships were named to travel to the port in which the vessel resided (in this case, Newport News, Virginia) to christen it. In mid-1902, Henry Teller, the senior senator from Colorado, chose the daughter of millionaire Thomas F. Walsh, a mining tycoon who had homes in both Washington, DC and the Centennial State. Teller did this because the then-governor of Colorado had no daughter.

Senator Teller did not take into account that a gubernatorial election in November 1902 might bring a new governor and family into the capitol and indeed, it did. Republican James Peabody succeeded Democrat Teller, and his eldest daughter, Cora, desperately wanted to be the one to christen the warship. The Colorado legislature did not wish to offend the Walshes by rescinding the offer to their daughter, nor did it wish to risk Governor Peabody's pulling back the allocated funds for the event. When the legislature settled an amount for the exhibit budget, it also raised the number of commissioners from five to seven. In this way, it could appoint Mr. Walsh as one of them, with the understanding that his daughter would decline her christening duties, which she did graciously. Both the sixth and the seventh spots added were intended to give a Republican majority on the commission; as it originally stood, three of the five original members were Democrats.[12]

With six spots spoken for, the seventh needed to be assigned very carefully. "The appointment of the seventh member threatened another social war," wrote the *Inter Ocean*, "when the women of Colorado decided that they should have a representative on the board. Upon this announcement, friends of Mrs. Leonel Ross Anthony started a campaign for her appointment." And Campbell lobbied hard for it. After all, she had written a number of supportive articles for Governor Peabody during his campaign. The governor may have thought Campbell had proven her mettle with the St. John affair, given that he tended to side against labor in matters of unrest. But most important, Campbell had many confidants in the state assembly, both Republican and Democrat. "She was not favored by all the representatives of her sex," continued the *Inter Ocean*, "but had many friends in the Legislature, and in the end it appeared that the bill could not pass unless it was tacitly understood that Mrs. Anthony would be appointed." Thus, the $100,000 appropriation bill for the fair was passed, and Campbell was added to the directorate.[13]

"By native ability, personality, opportunity and training, she will be able to serve the interests of the state as no other woman in the state, and few men, could do. Not only by her pen, which as an advertising medium of the resources of the Silver States will be unrivalled, but by the social connections in the East and the South which will make the work of a commissioner from a western state more easily productive of result."[14] This unsourced quote in a press release may in fact have come from Campbell herself. Yet for all the trouble the writer went through to gain such a plum assignment, she spent precious little time working for the fair except to show up at the obligatory meetings and plan a couple of trips to St. Louis for the following spring. Campbell was about to launch a venture that was much more personally fulfilling.

Photo of Nell Campbell as a young woman, in the early 1880s, taken in St. Louis.

Side profile portrait of Nell Campbell in her thirties, taken at the Fredericks Knickerbocker photography studio in New York City, where wealthier families and aspiring actresses often went for publicity photos.

Strauss

Photo of Nell Campbell as a young adult, in the early 1880s, taken in St. Louis, around the time of her marriage to George Anthony Jr. This may have been a honeymoon portrait.

Against the advice of friends and the superintendent of the Cheesman Dam construction, Nell Campbell, "Polly Pry," allowed herself to be hoisted more than 200 feet in the air to get a good look at the progress of this work abutting the South Platte River. The headline for the *Denver Post* article that featured this stunt was "Polly Pry's Deed of Daring" (September 15, 1901, 15).

Studio portrait of Nell Campbell, taken in New York City, circa 1895. This was likely a publicity photo she sent to directors and producers when auditioning for theatrical roles.

Full-figured portrait of Nell Campbell, taken in Denver for her *Polly Pry* magazine debut (1903).

Full-figured portrait of Nell Campbell, circa 1905. This may be a bridal photo taken for her marriage to Harry O'Bryan.

Polly Pry's home on Colfax Street, Denver. In January 1904, after an unknown assailant attempted to shoot her in her own doorway, newsboys from all over the city offered to keep watch at her home.

Nell Campbell in her early twenties, posing for what was likely an acting portfolio or advertisement for her part in a play.

"Cannibal" Alfred Packer. Polly Pry's articles about Packer's prolonged imprisonment spurred the governor of Colorado to parole him in February 1901. Packer was convicted in 1874 of murdering his fellow prospectors. He admitted to eating some of their remains to survive the harsh cold.

Convicted assassin Tom Horn. Nell Campbell wrote many columns urging the citizens of Wyoming to consider that Horn was a pawn of powerful cattle barons.

A cartoon that appeared in the debut issue of the magazine *Polly Pry*, September 5, 1903. The figure of Nell Campbell and her weekly appear to be a calm and rational alternative to the other news outlets available in Denver at that time. Note that her old boss, Harry Tammen, is portrayed as Napoleon.

THE DENVER PUBLIC LIBRARY, WESTERN HISTORY PHOTOGRAPHIC COLLECTIONS

Nell Campbell was always a style icon, even as she approached middle age. (Photo circa 1910.)

Nell Campbell pins a poppy on a Denver gentleman, while other Red Cross workers watch. On "Poppy Day," in May 1921, Campbell helped raise hundreds of thousands of dollars for suffering children in war-torn Europe.

Pen and ink drawing made of Nell Campbell just before she died in 1938. The artist is unknown.

SIGNING THE PAPERS FOR THE WORLD TITLE MATCH

New York and Chicago have nothing on Denver when it comes to the promotion by women of big athletic events for the benefit. of war victims. Therefore, Polly Pry and the American Legion will stage a monster wrestling carnival and patriotic meeting at the municipal Auditorium next Monday night for the American and French Children's league. Three state champion grapplers and one world's champ are on the program, their services being free. The photo shows Champion Clarence Eklund, king of the light heavyweights, signing a contract to appear Monday night, with Polly Pry, promoter of the event, looking on. Standing, left to right, are Cy Mitchell, Sheridan promoter and sport authority, and McEvoy and Tally, matchmakers, who secured the talent. Eklund will defend his title against Jack Hunnel, Arizona demon, while Toots Mondt, Colorado champion, and George Nelson, Utah chieftain, will appear in another match. All the wrestlers are in Denver today putting the finishing touches to their training for Monday night's battles.

Polly Pry would do just about anything to raise awareness and funds for the causes she believed in. Here, she signs a contract for a wrestling match that was held in May 1921 between several Western state champions to raise money for the American and French Children's League.

THE DENVER PUBLIC LIBRARY, WESTERN HISTORY PHOTOGRAPHIC COLLECTIONS

A young Harry Heye Tammen, co-owner of the *Denver Post* from 1894 until his death in 1924.

Nell Campbell, "Polly Pry," (fur collar) is shown here as director of information for the American Relief Committee to Greece. With her is Miss Mary F. Pratt of Wheeling, West Virginia, a field secretary, also assigned to work with the Committee to Greece. They were photographed at the Red Cross headquarters in London in 1918.

CHAPTER 7

Tell the Truth and Shame the Devil

Nell Campbell and Frances Benson met when both were still married and living in New York. Benson's husband, Theodor Chominski, was twice his wife's age and a well-known painter and book illustrator. Before she met Chominski, Benson had come to New York alone in the early 1890s, with no professional experience but a desire to work in the newspaper world. Her first story was about her trip to Coney Island on a floating hospital. When the afternoon daily did not send her payment for the story nor the offer of employment she'd hoped for, Benson knocked on the doors of the publisher and would not leave until she got both. "Pretty, young and brave she is, and with a vim and go that few men have, and with a rare executive ability added to undeniable cleverness and industry, she could not fail," said one syndicated newspaper article of her in 1893. In 1896, Benson left her job as sole editor of *The Queen of Fashion* magazine to join the editorial staff of *Vogue*.[1]

It seems that Benson left her husband at some point, because by 1902 she was living in Denver with an uncle and writing for the *Rocky Mountain News*; later, she worked as a stenographer for Colorado's World's Fair committee. In early June of 1903, Campbell, Benson, and a printer named J. E. Hutchinson walked into the offices of the city clerk and incorporated themselves as "The Polly Pry Publishing Company." Campbell set up desks at her home at 131 West Colfax Avenue and purchased second-hand printing machinery. She employed many young men and women to sell advertising and hired former colleague Winifred Sweet Black (Annie Laurie) to help her produce the paper.

The first issue of *Polly Pry* was delivered to 3,500 subscribers on September 5, 1903. It was a hybrid of newspaper and magazine, one of only a few founded and run by a woman at this time, so the event was noticed by other sheets far and wide. One said, "A brand new debutante is about to be presented to the journalistic world. It comes from out of the West and its dress for the important first appearance is described by a Western daily as 'pink, a lovely rose color,' and 'very artistic.'" The description of its cover was not as positive: "The trimmings of the dress, according to the daily aforesaid, include a bizarre border, a triangle of grotesque faces in one corner peering down at a feminine figure in the opposite corner, and the words 'Polly Pry' written across the page, with 'characteristic dash.'" This wasn't quite accurate, though the cover did feature a sketch of a fancy-hatted woman's large head staring at the reader from behind a spiderweb.[2]

Campbell promised her subscribers that *Polly Pry* would consist of a wide range of things to read: society, wit, humor, and current events. It would have a page devoted to a new apparatus then making headlines: the automobile. Each issue would contain an article about sports, and of course, it would contain society announcements of all kinds. "About one-half of the paper will be devoted to politics," Campbell said, "and all questions affecting the people will be fully presented and impartially discussed." Depending on space, Campbell added, there would be theatrical gossip, financial news, and one or more short fiction stories.[3]

A friend from the *Post* wrote of Campbell's hard work and new venture:

> *Then there are others who win by waiting, who take fortune at the precise flood, and have the gift of knowing exactly how, when and where to strike. For example, there is Polly Pry. She has long dreamed of owning and editing a periodical which will be her ideal—bright, keen, earnest, good natured and typographically attractive. She firmly believed Denver was the exact field for such a venture and she has talked about it long and frequently. I have listened to her plans for a year or two with interest, but not mad enthusiasm. There is nothing more deadly to me than a "long felt want," and I really couldn't see the primrose path of the fair Polly's proposition. "It will require plenty of money, an indefatigable publisher, more than one set of brains and continuous pushing to succeed," I coldly observed. "I know it," she*

*answered, "and yet my dream will be realized and the periodical made
a success."... She talked her plan to the prosperous, who are somewhat
bookishly inclined. They listened, were converted, liberally subscribed
and within ten days after she began her real effort the clever lady put
$15,000 in solid cash in the First National bank.... They say you can
get anything you want if you wish hard enough, and Polly not only
wished, but acted.... There is a homely maxim, of something more
than indifferent wisdom, saying, "If you have a cow you can have a
cow given you," and Mrs. Anthony having gotten the attention and
the ear of the rich can now produce something quite worthwhile, and
I'll be bound she will.[4]*

Many local papers lauded *Polly Pry* when it came out. The *Colorado
Transcript* in Golden compared it to some New York papers, noting that
its advertising space was "well-filled" and predicting that it would be a
"howling financial success." The *Yuma Pioneer* said it was "neatly gotten
up" and that the matter lying between the attractive covers of the magazine was the unvarnished truth, with "t's all crossed and i's all dotted."
Polly Pry, said the *Ouray Plaindealer*, was a "fearless and independent"
journalist, and that her work was all "well written with keen satire and
with such ability that the paper will soon be a welcome visitor in every
gentleman's office or fireside."

Of course, some regional newspapers weren't as kind with their
reviews. Leadville's *Herald Democrat* wondered—since *Polly Pry* sold out
of its first issue—who bought up all the copies? And the *Telluride Journal*
wrote that her discussion of state supreme court nominees was "light
and airy," about as nutritious as angel food cake. Some, like the *Salida
Record*, hedged their bets: "The infant is not particularly strong, but it has
a chance to grow. The press work is done on good paper, while some of the
artistic features are fairly good, but the makeup would give a good printer
or methodical journalist with an eye for the artistic and general fitness of
things a nightmare."[5]

There is no record of where and when Campbell held the reception
for the inauguration of her paper, but the *Post* may have gotten wind of
the many regrets sent along by those in dramatic, literary, and journalistic

circles. Still, Campbell's former employer gave a perfunctory report of the upcoming event:

> *While the "christening" of "Polly Pry" Sunday evening for which Mrs. Leonel Ross Anthony has issued invitations may not be a silver cup ceremony, it is sure to be a brilliantly novel event. The godmother, Mrs. Anthony, by reason of her cleverness and proverbial good luck stands practically like "Robinson Crusoe of old, monarch of all she surveys," among Denver's press writers who united in wishing success to "Polly Pry," whether in person or in print.[6]*

The issues were divided up into four rough categories: "The Midway," which would discuss political matters related to Denver and Colorado; "The Play," which would consist of reviews of local stage productions; "The Automobile," which would devote space to anything new about the new mechanical vehicles; and what may have been her most popular column, "Tell Truth and Shame the Devil."

"Shame the Devil" was a gossip column that—as Sue Hubbell wrote—was delicious to read even if one had never even heard of the people discussed: "Senator Carey has cut son Bobby off with a shilling and all because he married Julia Freeman, daughter of General Freeman, U.S.A. Now Bobby will have to work overtime, too, for Julia has tastes not at all compatible with the love in a cottage idea."[7] Even by modern standards, Campbell's written observations would be considered especially acerbic. She pointed her pen at celebrities:

> *Mrs. Buffalo Bill! Ah, well, she has been Mrs. Buffalo Bill a long time. She was poor with him out on the ranch in Wyoming, and the winds out there do play the very dickens with a woman's complexion. It's rather a pity, as she has borne him two daughters and has always worshiped the ground he busts bronchos on. But still——.*

At city employees:

> *What is to happen to the firemen on duty who let exit doors be locked night after night and day after day, without saying a word about it?*

What will be done with the arch criminals—the men who schemed and planned to evade just and reasonable ordinances for the provision of public safety, until disaster caught hundreds of victims in one of their nets, and so exposed the others? . . . In all these years there has been but one theater in town which made even a pretense of adequate protection against fire—the Tabor—the Curtis and the cheaper theaters, tinder boxes and death traps all of them. . . . They ought to have put a death's head and cross bones on these playhouses by way of a decoration and a prophecy.

Even at customer service at the local library:

The real book lovers don't go to the Library any more. There's no browsing among volumes, no loitering over some book which, picked up by chance, reveals a new world of delightful surprises. It's having your little slip made out, like an election ballot, and walking up to the window and apologetically asking one of the maids or William boys who abound to get you one of the books you desire. When the book is brought you receive it as though your name was Fido instead of Mrs. Jones.[8]

Campbell made an announcement at the beginning of her first issue. She said that contrary to what had been written about her endeavor, no millionaires contributed money to it and certainly not $15,000. She said that one can usually get what one wants in the world if one wishes for it hard enough and at the same time hustles. "It is not exactly a howling beauty," she wrote, "but for that you can blame my 'millionaire friends,' it is as lovely as I could afford to make it, that is my first and only apology. The contents I am responsible for." She recalled some advice she once got from a New York editor. "Tell the story as it is," he said, "and remember, on this paper you are not to have any veneration for anybody or anything except God—and—well—you might temper that a little."[9]

Two days after *Polly Pry* debuted, the *Aspen Daily Times* wrote of Campbell: "She says in her opening announcement that 'no one except the frauds, the shams, hypocrites and evil doers need fear it.' If she makes all of those four classes fear it in Denver she has her work cut out for her.

But she is in the right track, and if she will but stick to it she may help greatly in making Denver cleaner and straighter than it has been for many a day." The keen insights of a smart woman, the article continued, was a power that was too often underestimated: "Stay with it, Polly; you're all right on the getaway."[10]

CHAPTER 8

Mining Wars, Murder, and Mother Jones, Part I

The man was small and wore a stiff hat. He moved forward and put his foot on the doorstep. "Is Mrs. Anthony at home?" he asked.

"What do you want?" replied Nell Campbell.

The man repeated the question, and Campbell repeated her own. She stood in the center of the doorway.

"I wanted to see about an ad," said the man.

"Come tomorrow and see Mr. Thompson," said Campbell, and with that she shut the door. She walked back into her dining room and into the butler's pantry.

"I'll fix some hot water," she said to her friend, reporter John Bell, "and you can have a hot toddy."

She lit the gas stove and was looking for some lemons when the doorbell rang a second time.

"Look out, now," Bell said, "I will go to the door."

"No, I will go," Campbell said, "You must keep out of the cold air."

She hurried to open the door, but sounded nervous when she asked who it was. The man on the other side of the door, William Walling, worked for an eastern labor magazine and was in Denver partly to visit family but primarily to collect information about the families of striking miners, and he wished to get Polly Pry's input. Walling laughed at her and said, "You must be afraid, if you demand to know the names of your callers before you answer the door."[1]

Campbell laughed at Walling's assessment and let down her guard a little bit. She had experienced some anxiety that afternoon and early evening. In those days, when people chose to advertise their wares or companies, they personally dropped off funds for ad placement in a newspaper or magazine. Campbell announced in the *Post* that she would accept advertising, but she neglected to say what time callers should come. Thus, about two dozen people had come to her house on that Sunday afternoon of January 10, 1904, while she was entertaining family and friends and had already sent her maid home for a day of rest.

The journalist's mother and father arrived at the Colfax Avenue home late in the afternoon, but Mary Campbell decided she wanted to leave and visit a nearby friend. Nelson Campbell accompanied his wife to the friend's home, as did John Bell, so he could walk back with the aging Mr. Campbell. When they arrived back at Nell's home, they were joined by her brother Roy and his first wife, friend, and business partner, Frances Benson, and a few others. Nelson Campbell felt ill, so his daughter and Benson escorted him up to the second floor to nurse him. The doorbell rang yet again. Nell ran downstairs to answer the door, and there was the strange little man who demanded to know if "Mrs. Anthony" was home. After shooing him away, the bell rang again. With a creeping feeling, Campbell opened the door while pressed to the left of the doorway instead of in her usual center stance.

Before the writer could peer further around the doorframe to see who was there, she was blinded by light and deafened by two gunshots. She screamed and stumbled toward the dining room. Bell came running from the butler's pantry and asked if she had been hurt. "I did not know," Campbell said, "I was so badly frightened." Brother Roy Campbell raced downstairs with his revolver and ran into the street, looking for the shooter. John and Frances "Pinky" Wayne also came running down from the second floor. Frances Benson, still tending to Nelson Campbell, thought the sounds were from dynamite and waited to see which way the house was going to fall down before starting on a run. Once she realized nothing was going to implode, she also raced downstairs but at the head of the stairway slipped and fell, badly spraining her ankle.[2] "Just an hour before," Benson said later, "I had told Mr. [Roy] Campbell to search the house. I had been afraid they would blow us up."

By "they," Benson was referring to the United Mine Workers of America (UMWA). Late in 1903, *Polly Pry* quickly ditched the social news that had dominated the initial issues of the magazine and became a hard-charging, anti-union instrument with most of its criticisms aimed at organized labor within the mining industry. Campbell thought that the shooting at her home might have been directly related to some printed sparring with John L. Gehr, head of the UMWA:

> *"In the previous issue I had made certain statements about him that he did not like. . . . He threatened me with legal action if I did not retract my statements. I refused to do this. I may be doing him a great injustice, but he has been in town for several days. But I will not discuss this phase of the case at the present time."*[3]

A reporter asked her if a member of society who felt that he or she had been unfairly maligned in the pages of *Polly Pry* might be responsible, but Campbell felt certain this was not possible: "For the past eight weeks I have had very little society matter," she said, "and then it is not strong enough, and people do not bother about this kind of matter anyhow. It is silly to even think that any society person would want to put me out of the way for some little thing I had written about them."[4]

Campbell did not get a good look at the shooter's face, owing to the fact that the entire lower floor of her home was darkened but for the light in the dining room, which did not reach the main entrance. She did, however, think that the man used a Winchester, because a "long sheet of flame" shot out from it. Had the bullets struck her, she thought, they would have entered right below her heart. As it happened, the first bullet struck the side of a writing desk and crashed into a wall. The second entered near the ceiling of a nearby room. When the police were able to dig out one of the bullets, they declared that it was fired from a .45-caliber gun. Campbell estimated that the shooter was tall, about six feet. And brother Roy and policeman Thomas Stack theorized that a man who was seen loafing around a widow's home about a block away from Campbell's house in the days before the attack might be responsible.

The Denver police were circumspect. Chief of police Hamilton Armstrong lamented that the agency had no clues to work on. "In my opinion they certainly intended to kill Polly Pry," he said. "We have men out West who would be willing to kill her or any newspaper man for the asking." Still, said Armstrong, all the police in the world could not protect somebody who was in the sights of someone who really wanted to kill him or her. "We will do all within our power to try to find the persons guilty. . . . I have my own ideas about the case, but to give them publicity would defeat the end for which we are working. I hope to have a talk with Mrs. Anthony during the day and, if our ideas agree, have a few arrests made. It wouldn't be surprising if we got the right man among half a dozen I suspect." The chief suspected that the shooter was merely a hired "tool."[5] Hattie Fox, Campbell's landlady, turned over a letter to her tenant the day after the shooting. She had received it a week prior; it said if Fox did not evict her renter, the house would be blown up.

Meanwhile, some members of the community rallied for Campbell's protection. General John Chase, head of the Colorado National Guard, called upon some twenty businessmen to take turns watching her house. A delegation of newsboys reported for duty as well, rotating every few hours. "Some of the gang will be around here all the time," the newsboys said, "selling our papers. And you can bet we will tip you off or put the police wise if we see anything wrong." Winifred Black, the other female *Denver Post* reporter, took out an ad in that paper to quit her job there in order to show solidarity with Campbell:

To the Editors of The Post:

Gentlemen—Up to this day I have been simply a contributor to Polly Pry. Now that the union men whom she has exposed in her paper seem to be trying to kill her, I wish to announce that I am connected with the paper and that I am willing to take my full share of responsibility. If there is any shooting to be done, the gentlemen who are handy with guns will find me at the Polly Pry office every day between 10 o'clock and 5.

It is time for the men and women of Denver who have one spark of American spirit left in their hearts to stand by Polly Pry and by the fight she is making for American liberty, American free speech and the right to live a fearless American life.

*Please publish this card prominently in your story of the attempted
assassination of Polly Pry. Yours faithfully,*
WINIFRED BLACK[6]

Not everyone believed Campbell's version of what happened that
evening. On Tuesday, January 12—two days after the alleged attempt on
Polly Pry's life—the *Rocky Mountain News* published its assessment of the
events equal to the *Post's* in length. It was scandalous, for it said that the
shots came from the gun of none other than Campbell's own guest, John
E. "Jack" Bell.

Just an hour before the shooting, Bell—head of the Victor, Colorado,
Independence Mine and occasional contributor to the *Post* and other
Western newspapers—paid a call to the local police station and retrieved
his revolver, which police had taken from him the night before when he
was drunk in public. The bullets pulled from the living room of Nell's
house looked suspiciously like the ammunition used in such a revolver.

Moreover, continued the *Mountain News* article, when Campbell's
friends rushed downstairs into her reception room after the shooting, it
was filled with a "blinding smoke" that was still there ten minutes later
when neighbor John Corbett was allowed in. And twenty minutes after
that, when police sergeant Frank Kratke and detectives R. W. White and
W. W. Arnett arrived, the room was still thick with smoke. "Such a con-
dition," said the *Mountain News*, "could not have existed, the officers say,
had the man who fired the shots stood out on the porch and shot through
an opening of eighteen inches as Mrs. Anthony declares." And, the article
continued, there were many pedestrians still out on the street at that early
nighttime hour—none of them saw the would-be assassin run away.
Almost all of the neighboring homes reported flinging open their windows
to see where the shots and screams came from but even with bright street
lights saw no one fleeing.[7]

Taking its analysis even further, the *Mountain News* printed that Nell
and Roy made some contradictory statements to the police and the public.
To Sergeant Kratke, Nell said she took the precaution of shielding herself
by standing behind the door when she opened it. But she told Detective

Arnett that she stood directly in the threshold when she first opened the door, but on second thought, fearing some sort of violence, stepped around behind the door. Both Nell and Roy said that Roy hurried down the stairs, pistol in hand, when he heard the shots and then ran out into the street to pursue the "murderous stranger." However, the detectives allegedly gleaned from others in the home that Roy never left the house. And the sound itself was suspect, argued the *Mountain News*, because anything that sounded as loud and crackling as dynamite meant that it had to be something shot from *inside* the house, not outside of it. And somehow the *Mountain News* gleaned that Hattie Fox, owner of Nell's house, never received a threatening letter at all.

Campbell's demeanor was suspect, too, according to the *Post*'s rival paper. When the first officers arrived, it said, she was not the least nervous or excited but became more animated and agitated as more and more people interviewed her.

When Campbell told officers the description of the man—six feet tall, with a dark mustache and a black derby hat—they deduced that it might be John L. Gehr, one of the leaders of the United Mine Workers of America. Others thought it might be Gehr, too. Harry Tammen visited Campbell shortly after the shooting and asked the detectives to arrest Gehr; they declined because they could not connect him with the crime.[8]

No one ever came to a firm conclusion about what really happened at Polly Pry's home the night of January 10, 1904. Campbell published an "Official Police Report" in her January 16 edition of *Polly Pry*, complete with statements by various detectives. The only additional information in the official report was that Campbell told them she thought the shooter was "tall and rather large, dark complexioned, with a moustache, wearing a derby hat."[9] The outcome was the same regardless of whether Campbell and her brother and friend Bell faked the shooting or whether it was a true attempt upon her life. The event brought even more attention to Campbell's vicious war of words with organized labor and in particular with a woman named Mary Harris "Mother" Jones.

Campbell's interest in Jones, the Western Federation of Miners (WFM), and the capitalists who owned the mines requires some historical context. The series of labor events that Polly Pry would either cover in her writings or be directly involved with spanned November 1903 to June 1904. But Colorado's era of industrial warfare really started in the early 1890s and stretched all the way through 1914. The bitterest of battles involving mine owners, processing-company owners, and the men who labored to bring ore out of the ground took place in Cripple Creek, just slightly southeast of the center of the state near Colorado Springs, where much of Colorado's ore was processed.

The Cripple Creek mining district lies on the southwestern flank of Pikes Peak, which is more than fourteen thousand feet high. Pikes is located in El Paso County and is one of the most eastern peaks in the Rocky Mountain Range. Thousands of would-be prospectors and miners—called 1859ers—flooded into the South Platte River region where shallow deposits of gold had been discovered near the present-day Denver suburb of Englewood. This "initial boom" created explosive population growth in the region, and within a few years, Denver City, Boulder City, and Golden City were substantial towns serving the mines. Without the technology to reach deeper ore, however, Cripple Creek miners finished extracting whatever they could within a few years and moved on to other deposits like those found in Telluride.

In 1890, ranch-hand-turned-prospector Bob Womack discovered deeper reserves in the region; by that time technology had caught up to the needs of mine owners. During the Panic of 1893, mine owners took advantage of thousands of unemployed men by restoring a ten-hour workday for the pay of an eight-hour day. The Western Federation of Miners, the dominant labor union in Aspen, had fought hard for the eight-hour day and immediately went on strike across the state. During a confrontation in Cripple Creek, Governor Davis H. Waite sided with the strikers. This position was a first for a governor, and it resulted in mine owners backing off. Over the next decade, the WFM gained strength and attempted to unionize smelters and related businesses. They also switched their battles from armed conflict to the ballot box. They won a statewide referendum that extended the eight-hour workday to many workers and also restored a guaranteed three-dollar-per-day wage for workers.

By 1900, five hundred mines had been opened, the towns of Cripple Creek and Victor had been established, and rail service had linked the district to the outside world. Gold production peaked around 1900 with a value of $18 million. From 1890 to 1910, 22.4 million ounces of gold were mined.[10] The district is noted for several large and famous mines and is said to have produced thirty millionaires.

As might be expected, these industrialists organized to banish unions. They elected Governor James Peabody, an anti-union Republican. After taking office in 1902, Peabody and the legislature ignored the eight-hour workday referendum. The larger mining companies began firing union employees. As the mine operators imported nonunion labor from outside the district, the union formed armed camps to barricade the roads and railroads leading into the fields. After an appeal to Governor Peabody, the mine owners welcomed an investigatory committee and, immediately afterward, on its recommendation, the governor dispatched the militia to Cripple Creek. In his inaugural address in 1903, Peabody had pledged to protect lives and property. Those sympathetic to labor, however, felt that he shared the business community's hostility toward the union and directed the power of his office against it.[11]

In 1904, the conflict between mine owners and miners led to the declaration of a state of insurrection in Teller County, the military occupation of the Cripple Creek district, the suspension of civil rights, the removal of elected officials, and the forced deportation of union miners and their sympathizers. More than thirty souls died in violence relating to the strike. Although the strike was initially about practical issues of wages and hours, it quickly became a philosophical and legal battle over the right of workers to organize and the right of owners to run their businesses as they saw fit. "The civil, military and constitutional conflicts that came out of the strike," writes labor historian Bridget Burke, "established Colorado as the birthplace of western labor radicalism and reinforced the state's reputation as a safe haven for western business conservatism."[12]

On November 21, 1903, a deadly event at the Vindicator gold mine in Cripple Creek made headlines. An explosion on the sixth level of the nonunion mine killed two men, and it was determined that it came from a bomb, even though the camp was well guarded at the time. The Cripple

Creek Mine Owners Association blamed the WFM—Campbell did too. Then, on January 26, 1904, fifteen men were killed when a strikebreaking engineer lost control of a cage engine. The strain on the cable caused it to break, releasing the cage and the miners down the shaft. Nell pulled at the heart strings of her readers:

> *The driving snow is falling on the narrow graves of the men who died down there in the dark, and the women and the little children have gone home—alone. And the worst horror of all the dreadful horrors that have turned our hearts to water in this fearful time is not the awful death of the helpless men down there at the bottom of the cruel shaft, not the wailing of the fatherless children, not the dry-eyed grief of the stricken women, but that you and I and the man who lives across the way, and the woman who lives next door, are all ready to ask . . . "Who has done this thing?"[13]*

Although the fifteen strike leaders who were arrested were never prosecuted, suspicions never pointed in any other direction.[14]

After an extended period of violent clashes between union and non-union groups, the WFM was driven from the Colorado mines in June of 1904. Campbell thrust herself and *Polly Pry* into a critical role in these violent clashes and reported heavily on the people involved in them.

Just after Thanksgiving in 1903, Campbell wrote this manifesto that appeared in her paper:

> *Polly Pry is the only paper in Colorado that dares print the truth about the strike situation, which is today the most serious thing that confronts all the people and interests of the State. Careful and conscientious investigation will be made by personal visits to the different sections where the trouble exists, and the truth will be told. The whole truth will be printed without the cowardly fear which causes the daily newspapers to shy at the actual condition and the causes which have brought about and keep up that condition. If you want to know the facts—whether you are a capitalist, a day-laborer, a union man, or simply one of the unfortunate individuals who must pay [severe]*

prices for the fuel to keep you warm, you will find these facts in Polly Pry and in no other paper.[15]

Indeed, the "strike situation" was the most serious thing that confronted many—if not all—people of Colorado and the surrounding states and territories. While Cripple Creek was indeed a center of rich gold ore, it was also rich in its community life. It certainly had the roughness of a mining camp, but it also had a thriving society with churches, schools, lodges and social organizations, cultural amenities, and a "stable, law-abiding citizenry."[16] It was, in 1903, the largest urban area in the state, with nearly forty thousand people. And unlike other mining camps with highly transient, mostly male populations, Cripple Creek residents included high percentages of women, families, and homeowners. These demographics, Burke writes, suggest that the Cripple Creek strike was not just a labor conflict—it was about competing visions of community. And as events got more serious in Cripple Creek at the end of 1903 and beginning of 1904, Campbell shifted *Polly Pry* from a gossip magazine to an anti-labor weekly, believing industrial conflict to be the most important issue facing the state and even the nation at large.

Campbell made it clear that she was no enemy of organized labor but that the WFM was made up of "a body of malcontents" who were a constant source of trouble and "antagonistic to the business interests of their employers and indifferent to the welfare of the community." Furthermore, Campbell wrote, the WFM was composed of men who incited riots and openly advocated for murder, assassination, and arson. She argued that unions made half the industries in Colorado lie idle and were responsible for the depreciation of property, for hundreds of men out of work, and for injuring the reputation of the State. She asked her readers what the union hoped to gain for all their trouble.

"To secure an eight-hour day? They have had it for years in both Cripple Creek and Telluride."

"Better wage? They are now paid higher wages than any other miners in the United States."

"What then? So far as any reasonable person can see they have no real complaint," she concluded.[17]

In fact, Campbell wrote, WFM did not care about its workers' welfare at all but rather used the coalition for a sinister purpose: to establish a "national headquarters for anarchists and revolutionary socialists" in the state of Colorado. She maintained that leaders J. C. Sullivan, William Haywood, Charles Moyer, and David C. Coates planned to install themselves as the "High Priests" of these monstrous political doctrines, so they could control the operations of Cripple Creek and Telluride.

Polly Pry reminded readers that she had been in Telluride two years before, after Arthur Collins had been "foully assassinated," so she knew full well what the WFM was capable of. She also took the opportunity to take a measure of revenge upon her previous employers, Tammen and Bonfils, or at least to get the last word on the subject of Vincent St. John: "Mr. St. John did not hesitate to express his views—either in regard to the murder of Mr. Collins, which was, according to his ideas, a mere meting out of justice, nor in regard to the necessity for the 'removal' of various other men, who . . . had become objectionable to the union."[18] Campbell shored up her labor reporting credentials by visiting and writing about outlying coal towns, iron suppliers, and labor organizers such as John Mitchell of the United Mine Workers, which represented primarily coal miners at this time versus the hard metal workers represented by WFM. She wrote about the differences between coal mining communities in Colorado and those in Pennsylvania, where the people lived close together and had a social life, amusements, and recreation. "Here," she noted of the coalfields in Colorado, miners "are isolated, cut off from the world. They are huddled together in badly arranged camps, housed like animals and treated like beasts of burden." Campbell recalled for her readers that she had once worked near Trinidad in Las Animas County where the southern coal deposits were located, so she knew how frightful the conditions could be (though she neglected to give detail on this time in her life away from Denver). And closer to home, Campbell recounted the "food strike" of May 1903, which involved retail clerks, restaurant workers, and teamsters, and the Denver smelter strikes.

Within a few months of the initial publication, Campbell had shifted *Polly Pry*'s contents so that at least half of it was dedicated to "industrial conflict," with the rest consisting of gossip, politics, theater, and World's

Fair notes.[19] Later, *Polly Pry* included reports on strikes from delivery boys to hearse drivers from correspondents in San Francisco, Chicago, New York, and Indianapolis. She promised, "Wherever there is a strike, our man will be on the spot."[20]

By the time of the shooting at her home on January 10, 1904, Polly Pry had no shortage of union adversaries—John Gehr was but one of many who might have decided to pay retribution for the scarring things she said about them in her paper. The December 26, 1903, issue of *Polly Pry* declared labor leaders to be "men usually of little or no education, less principle, and no consideration either for the people they are supposed to represent, or for society at large." It turns out that Campbell's scorn was directed at a particular woman labor leader, too: Mother Jones.

CHAPTER 9

Mining Wars, Murder, and Mother Jones, Part II

Mother Jones was one of the first people Campbell wrote about in her November 28, 1903, "industrial labor debut" edition of *Polly Pry*. Born in Cork, Ireland, in 1830, Jones immigrated to the United States in about 1840, after her father had gained his citizenship. As a young woman she drifted to Michigan, where she taught in a Catholic school, then to Chicago, where she was a dressmaker, and finally to Memphis, where she met and married ironworker George Jones. In Memphis in the late 1860s, yellow fever killed her husband and all four children. These unspeakable tragedies shaped what she decided to do with the rest of her life. Grief-stricken, Jones moved back to Chicago, where, as a seamstress for the rich, she bitterly noted the contrast between the "luxury and extravagance" of the few and the misery of the "poor, shivering wretches" she saw on the streets.[1]

As if her ill fortune up to that point were not enough, in 1871 the Great Chicago Fire destroyed all of Jones's possessions. She could have fallen into depression, but instead, grief became the crucible of her commitment to working-class reform. Having lost her real family, she found a new one—the family of the oppressed and dispossessed. In the late 1870s, she experienced what she called a "conversion" to labor activism. With alarm, she bore witness to many of the strikes that swept the United States over the next two decades. Around 1900, she became the chief speaker for the United Mine Workers (UMW), the largest and most progressive union in the nation, and appeared not only at coal strikes, but at railroad, steel, textile, and brewery strikes as well.[2]

In 1903, Mother Jones began a dramatic crusade for a national child labor law, in Kensington, Pennsylvania, where seventy-five thousand textile workers were on strike for more pay and shorter hours; ten thousand of them were young children. She describes the scene in her autobiography: "Every day little children came into Union Headquarters, some with their hands off, some with the thumb missing, some with their fingers off at the knuckle. They were stooped little things, round-shouldered and skinny. Many of them were not over ten years of age, although the state law prohibited their working before they were twelve years of age." The law was poorly enforced. In many families, the father had been killed or disabled by work in the nearby coal mines. To feed the family, the mothers had to send their young children to work to get money for food. When Mother Jones asked local papers to publish the facts about child labor in Pennsylvania, they refused, saying the mill owners had stock in their newspapers. "Well, I've got stock in these children," she said, "and I'll arrange a little publicity."

In July of 1903, Mother Jones marched with a band of striking children from Pennsylvania to New York to meet with President Theodore Roosevelt and ask for his support for federal legislation to protect children. He denied her request to meet, and so Jones turned her attention to Colorado and the plight of coal mining families there. She arrived in Denver on Monday, October 19, and the next day made her way to the Coronado Hotel in Trinidad, where she held meetings at the office of the Western Federation of Miners. Once satisfied that she understood the plight of coal miners in both northern and southern Colorado, she disguised herself as a peddler and spent nights eating and sleeping at the homes of mining families. In her autobiography, she wrote that she had never seen such deplorable conditions:

> *They were in practical slavery to the company, which owned their houses, owned all the land, so that if a miner did own a house he must vacate whenever it pleased the land owners. They were paid in scrip instead of money so that they could not go away if dissatisfied. They must buy at company stores and at company prices. The coal they mined was weighed by an agent of the company and the miners could*

not have a check weighman to see that full credit was given them. The schools, the churches, the roads belonged to the Company. I felt, after listening to their stories, after witnessing their long patience, that the time was ripe for revolt against such brutal conditions.[3]

Jones went back to Trinidad on or around November 5 and spoke at length with WFM officials. "We sat up and talked the matter over far into the night. I showed them the conditions I had found down in the mining camps were heart-rending, and I felt it was our business to remedy those conditions and bring some future, some sunlight at least into the lives of the children," she wrote. They deputized her to go at once to headquarters in Indianapolis, where she convinced WFM president John Mitchell that conditions for coal workers in Colorado were untenable. He agreed, authorized her to return there, and said they would call a strike of the coal miners.

The WFM called its strike on November 9, 1903. The demands were for an eight-hour day, a check weighman representing the miners, payment in money instead of scrip. "The whole state of Colorado was in revolt," Jones recalled. "No coal was dug. November is a cold month in Colorado and the citizens began to feel the pressure of the strike."[4] The Vindicator mine explosion and complaints from mine owners and other prominent capitalists were too much fodder for Campbell to ignore, and she placed her anger toward organized labor squarely on the person who represented what she deemed the worst aspects of it—Mary Jones:

"Mother" Jones—mother of idleness and want and misery! God send us barrenness of motherhood if such as Jones be the alternative. Were there not enough home-grown noxious fungi to poison the Colorado miner's Thanksgiving broth that foreign toadstools must be imported? Have not the domestic assassins and dynamiters made Unionism such a reproach that an honest man hides his badge and hangs his head in shame?

Campbell wrote about the susceptibility of immigrants to someone who was, according to her, giving them permission not to work. "Striking miners up there—a motley collection of filthy, [illegible], uncouth, igno-rant foreigners. Italians, Huns, [illegible], Slavs, etc.—have a Soup House, where they congregate three times a day to feed—no other word could describe their performance." Jones, according to Polly Pry, knew exactly how to agitate a crowd of miners: "I would rather fight than work any day, wouldn't you, boys?" Jones had allegedly said to a group of them in Cripple Creek.[5]

"The real attraction," wrote Campbell when describing a meeting of union labor and its sympathizers to be held in Denver's coliseum on January 3, 1904, "is 'Mother' Jones, national labor agitator, about whom everybody is curious—which is why the following story may be of interest." She related some benign facts about Jones's biography up to the time Jones left Oyster Bay, New York, after being rebuffed by President Roosevelt. But then Campbell detailed some of the salacious details she had recently discovered about Mother Jones from a file at the local Pinkerton office:

> —*A vulgar, heartless, vicious creature, with a fiery temper and a cold-blooded brutality rare even in the slums.*
> —*An inmate of Jennie Rogers' house on Market street, Denver, some twelve years ago. She got into trouble with the Rogers woman for bribing all of her girls to leave her and go to a house in Omaha—for which act she was paid a procuress fee of $5 to $10 apiece for the girls.*
> —*She was a confidential servant in Rose Lovejoy's private house on Market street, Denver, and was with her several years.*
> —*A sewing woman for the sporting class living on Lawrence street— name withheld—knew her twelve or fifteen years ago, when she lived with Minnie Hall, and afterwards was a procuress by trade.*[6]

In other words, Mother Jones was a madam. With sarcasm, Campbell warned her readers not to be shocked at anything Jones might do or say, for she could "give a sailor points and beat him at his own game in the profanity line; and, as for vulgarity, she can discount the most hardened habitué of the lowest tenderloin dive."[7]

Journalistic reaction to the *Polly Pry* charges against Mother Jones was predictable, according to biographer Elliott Gorn. Anti-union newspapers reprinted the story; pro-union organs were outraged. Although the accusations probably were nothing more than slander, they underscore again the enigma of Mother Jones's past. Whether true or false, *Polly Pry*'s story hit a nerve. "All of the wholesome feelings," writes Gorn, "evoked by the legend of Mother Jones were inverted by the image of mother as a brothel keeper. If Mother Jones drew power from her purity, her enemies found a way of making the Madonna into a whore."[8]

Polly Pry's enemies used the same tactic against her. In March of 1904, Carlo Demolli, a paid organizer for the United Mine Workers of America (UMWA), decided he had had enough of Campbell's insults. In her January and February issues of *Polly Pry*, Campbell had targeted Demolli by name, accusing him of having fled Naples to avoid a prison sentence and of being a member of the Mafia. Outraged at such tactics and charges, Demolli chose to beat Pry at her own game, submitting his first letter to *Il Lavoratore Italiano*, an official newspaper of the UMWA's District 15, which served coal camps in Colorado, eastern Utah, southern Wyoming, and New Mexico. He claimed that he had recently met Pry in a Denver saloon and that Pry told him she was "a libertine and prostitute" as well as a successful journalist. Demolli then indicated that he asked Pry if he could "insert an ad in her paper for $2," a transaction he claimed was soon completed in her bedroom on Market Street. "Miserable!" he wrote, referring to her anti-union work. "Go back to your brothel house of Market Street and maybe there you can earn your life more 'honestly.'"[9] In October 1904, Demolli was convicted of sending obscene materials through the mail and spent two years at Leavenworth prison.

The Colorado Federation of Labor (CFL) planned a large meeting at Denver's coliseum hall for the evening of January 3, 1904, where many speakers would be allowed to present their opinions about the policy of Governor Peabody in sending militia to strike zones. CFL's attorneys, politicians and judges from affected counties, and Mother Jones were scheduled to speak. Polly Pry encouraged Coloradoans to attend this big gathering because they should heed "even the ridiculous statements" of "this infamous old woman," if only because she had so many supporters. The reporter urged all to attend who agreed with her that "anarchists and socialists of the entire country" were making desperate efforts to establish their headquarters in Colorado, or else Colorado would be in more trouble than anyone dreamed. WFM delegates John F. O'Neil, Charles Moyer, Bill Haywood, and, of course, Jones and her followers needed to be "put down and put down now," Campbell said.[10]

The words "put down and put down now" were aimed at Governor Peabody and his National Guard adjutant general, Sherman Bell, who was the military commander in the Cripple Creek district. Mine owners begged Peabody to send more troops into various strike zones to protect nonunion workers who had taken the place of the striking employees.[11] Judge Frank W. Owers, who presided over the Fifth Judicial District of Colorado, including the mining town of Leadville, was at the coliseum rally and delivered a long resolution that Governor Peabody and his military rule should be stopped. Representatives from his district and the neighboring Fourth District threatened to bring suit against Peabody for using such heavy-handed tactics against men who were simply trying to better their standard of living.

Campbell attended the meeting and hired a few policemen to guard her. "It was expected," said the *Denver Post* the next day, "that 'Mother' Jones would have things to say to 'Polly Pry.'" But Jones was not there, having sent a telegram to colleagues to speak on her behalf because she was "indisposed."[12] Campbell may have been disappointed at first, but she took advantage of Jones's absence to denigrate her further, likening her no-show to a failure for "her children": "She will continue to fail them! Her throne is vacant—her position is 'to let.'" For good measure, Campbell threw in a few paragraphs about Jones's previous life as an alcoholic and gambler. Jones never publicly said why she was not at the coliseum, but since she was diagnosed with pneumonia a few days later, it's probable that she was already unwell.

Campbell did not stop at Jones's allegedly scandalous history. She accused the older woman of mismanaging union funds and outright theft at the expense of the very people she purported to help:

Every man who gives of his hard-earned pay to the support of his striking brothers, has a right to know what becomes of his money—I wonder how he likes the knowledge that his chosen leaders have been

deliberately misappropriating the funds—raised by his heartbreaking
toil, and given to aid a distressed comrade—and using them for their
own private enrichment?[13]

Even by Campbell's standards, the complete evisceration of Jones's character and motivations was extreme. It surely did not help that Jones was Irish and Catholic, which was in and of itself a category that Leonel Ross Campbell would dismiss out of hand unless a member had a lot of other "redeeming" qualities. Most definitely, Jones's ability to persuade thousands—millions, really—of people to take notice of the horrible plight of some workers was intimidating for Campbell, and she may have envied Jones's charisma.

But Campbell's fear of socialism in Colorado was real, and wherever it came from, it deeply influenced her to fiercely defend what she perceived as an assault on the rights of property owners.[14]

In late 1904, Campbell gave an interview to *American Industries* magazine. Though it was an anti-labor periodical and biased, it is nonetheless the most intimate explanation there is for the reasons she became so involved in the labor struggles of Colorado. She explained that she initially had no interest in making *Polly Pry* a labor paper, but "having taken some seven or eight months before a stand concerning events in one of the mining camps," she felt it necessary to explain her position. This was a reference to the Vincent St. John affair and the opportunity she took with her own paper to explain away what was surely an embarrassing situation with Tammen and Bonfils firing her instead of supporting her. But according to Campbell, this personal explanation opened her eyes to the "entire labor situation in parts of Colorado." It was not a pleasant experience, she said, and she had never before taken up a fight where she did not feel completely in touch with the working people—the "under dog." No, her fight was only with those who took advantage of a hardworking man—"professional agitators." In fact, *American Industries* claimed, Polly Pry had the friendship of union labor and plenty of letters from members to prove it.[15]

The crackdown continued; WFM leader Charles Moyer was arrested on charges of desecrating the American flag. In February 1904, the federation's leaders had printed broadsides with the flag on them, complete with a list of military abuses committed by Governor Peabody, Sherman Bell, the Colorado Citizens' Alliance (people opposed to employers who struck deals with unions), and smaller groups of "hired guns," like retired policemen and Pinkerton detectives. The poster also contained the image of a Telluride striker handcuffed to a telephone pole. Some of the statements in the stripes of the flag read,

> *"Martial law declared in Colorado!"*
> *"Wholesale arrests without warrant in Colorado!"*
> *"Union men exiled from homes and families in Colorado!"*

When Haywood and Moyer asked the question "Is Colorado in America?" they based their query on the assumption of basic rights—free speech, free press, the right to bear arms, trial by jury, and so on—rights that were legally and collectively embraced as core American values.[16]

Campbell asked the same question but framed it in terms of capitalism. In response to news of nonunion miners under armed guard for their protection, she asked in one of her editions of *Polly Pry*, "And this is in Free Colorado?" Would "the affairs of the United States be controlled by Americans or by labor unions?" she asked in another. When detailing the harassment of scabs in Cripple Creek, the shooting of a mine manager in Telluride, or the adoption of the socialist platform by the WFM, "And this is in Free Colorado?" was Polly Pry's refrain. She brought suit against Moyer for desecrating the flag, though it was quickly dismissed.

In February 1904, while attending a convention of the Citizens' Industrial Association in Indianapolis with Frances Benson, Campbell announced that she felt so strongly about thwarting "boycotts, anarchy and socialism" that she was looking for business partners who could help her start newspapers in Chicago and New York, and perhaps some in other cities as well for the main purpose of defeating "labor agitators and leaders that declare for boycotting and kindred troubles." Similarly, the goal of the Citizens' Industrial Association—better known as the Citizens' Alliance—was to isolate and boycott businesses that used unionized labor.[17]

In March of 1904, as miners' delegates met to discuss ending the strike, Governor Peabody declared martial law in the strike regions of the state. Undeterred, and no doubt relishing the challenge, Mother Jones returned after recovering from her illness. She spoke to striking miners in Trinidad on March 24, urging them to continue the fight and bolstering their morale. Two days later, she and four other leaders were arrested and placed on a train bound for La Junta, some sixty-five miles to the northeast, and told to stay away from the strike zone. Predictably, Mother Jones refused to keep her distance. She traveled from La Junta to Denver, taunting Governor Peabody about her presence in the state capital and broadcasting her intention to return to the southern mining region.[18]

Nell's accusations against Jones, Gehr, Moyer, and their associates were part of a much larger deterioration of the situation in Colorado. "Though the coal strike dragged on for almost a year," Gorn summarizes, "its end is quickly told." Divisions between conservative unionists and radicals, between local and national unions all widened. Led by dedicated organizers, the foreign miners remained stalwarts to the end; their families and communities became bastions of union strength. Mother Jones praised them in her autobiography: "No more loyal, courageous men could be found than those southern miners, scornfully referred to by 'citizens' alliances' as 'foreigners.' Italians and Mexicans endured to the end. . . . Theirs was the victory of the spirit."[19]

But solidarity was expensive; the UMWA treasury hemorrhaged funds for food, shelter, and transportation out of the strike zone for workers—not just the expenses of organizers like Mother Jones, as much as Polly Pry urged the public to believe that. When it was over, the strike had cost the union half a million dollars.[20]

Decades later, Bill Haywood wrote of Campbell and Mother Jones in his autobiography: "A notorious magazine, called Polly Pry's Magazine, printed a frightful tirade against Mother Jones. John Mitchell of the United Mine Workers seemed to think that there was some truth in the things that were written, and to his lasting disgrace, he discharged Mother Jones as an organizer, after all the brave work she had done for the miners of West Virginia, Pennsylvania, and elsewhere. I was glad to get her as an organizer for the WFM. She worked for us a short time during the Cripple Creek strike, but then took up her work among the coal miners again."[21]

Somewhere, somehow Campbell gleaned the nefarious plans of union leaders to get her to stop writing about them. She printed some of their quotes in her January 9, 1904, issue of *Polly Pry*:

> *"We're going to get even with her, though. She's done us too much dirt. We'll fix her."*
>
> Mr. Haywood

> *"Where in h—— is Polly Pry getting her stuff about us fellows? We've got to shut her up, or she'll break the strike."*
>
> National Officer Mooney, Personal Representative of President Mitchell

> *"I don't care anything about the d—— magazine. Only I'm going up there and clean out the shop if they don't let me alone."*
>
> John L. Gehr

> *"The sooner such people as Polly Pry are killed the better it will be for the world."*
>
> Mother Jones

And the very next day, January 10, 1904, that unknown assailant tried to shoot Polly Pry.

CHAPTER 10

The Business of Polly Pry

Nell turned forty-five in 1904. During an era in which most people her age might be slowing down, the writer was busier than she had ever been and was taking on more and more personal and professional responsibilities every day. With her increased workload and attempts to run a profitable business, Campbell found her career at odds with her social life more than ever and sometimes sought support in the unlikeliest of places.

Earlier in 1904, Campbell had convinced her fellow *Post* colleague Winifred Sweet Black to join *Polly Pry* at least on a freelance basis; Black became a full-time employee after the alleged attempt on Nell's life in January. Known more popularly as "Annie Laurie," Black was ten years younger than Campbell, but they had a lot in common. Like Nell, she was born in a small farm town, and like Nell, she had had a failed marriage before embarking on a journalistic career under the auspices of a yellow journalism czar—in Winifred's case, she was first hired by William Randolph Hearst before heading West to work for Tammen and Bonfils.

Having Black on *Polly Pry* was a coup for Nell. In addition to her investigative reporting credentials, she was a best-selling book author and well respected in Denver social circles. Additionally, she was married to Charles Bonfils, brother of Frederick Bonfils, although preferred to keep the pen name Winifred Black. It seems, though, that Black may have expected Campbell to run major staffing changes by her, or at least solicit her opinion. Perhaps Black had invested some money in *Polly Pry*, or perhaps she merely expected that Campbell would ask her advice because of her experience. In any case, Campbell caused a major rift between herself and her colleague when she hired a swindler and felon to act as a business manager for *Polly Pry*.

Harry Silberberg, who styled himself as "J. Coleman Drayton," was an established con man. He made a decent and legitimate living in the advertising business as a young man but found himself in enormous debt as his gambling habit overpowered him. In 1891, he caught "Mexican fever" and traveled to Chihuahua, where he thought he might start fresh but instead found himself in even more debt. He almost got away with $25,000 from a telegraph scheme, but he was intercepted by Mexican authorities before he could return to the states. While under house arrest at the home of a wealthy Chihuahuan official, Silberberg learned to type and speak Spanish before finally being allowed to return home. He spent the next ten years or so passing himself off as a relative of the Astors and marrying every young, wealthy heiress he could find in Europe and the United States. By the time he contacted Campbell in 1904, he had successfully absorbed the identity of the real J. Coleman Drayton, a wealthy New York attorney who was, in fact, married to a daughter of William Astor.[1]

On April 23, 1904, the *Colorado Springs Gazette* printed a scandalous story about "J. C. Drayton" and his attempt to swindle Mrs. Beulah Trimble Edwards, daughter of a Leadville millionaire. The day before, Silberberg called Edwards to make an appointment with her, stating that he had a "matter of some importance" that could only be discussed in person. He arrived at her residence in a handsome brougham carriage, drawn by a beautiful pair of high-stepping horses, and wearing the sharpest of tailor-made suits. After being seated in the parlor, he told Beulah the real reason for his visit, which was that as the new society editor of *Polly Pry*, he could, for the sum of $1,000, give a version of her pending divorce that was favorable to her side instead of that of her husband. He laughed when Edwards told him she had heard enough because he stated that he knew she had "$3,000,000 in her pocketbook on all occasions and would never miss a $1,000 bill."

Needless to say, Edwards was humiliated and, after getting rid of Silberberg immediately called the *Polly Pry* office. She learned that while the man was employed by the paper, he had not been sent to Colorado Springs, nor was the management aware that he had gone there. Unnamed sources at the *Polly Pry* office said that Campbell was on her way home from New York and had no knowledge of Silberberg's actions. Nell sent word that she would go straight to Chicago, where he was supposed to be going next, and file charges against him there.[2]

Campbell may have been trying to avoid some embarrassing revelations. A telegram from Winifred Black Bonfils reveals that Nell may have succumbed to the charms of someone she thought would be a financial and editorial boon to *Polly Pry*:

> *Dear Mrs. Anthony—*
>
> *I came down to the office this morning prepared to get the paper out till you came; but your telegram has put the whole matter on an entirely different footing. You put a man whom you know to be a self-confessed swindler, an ex-convict, in charge of your paper. When he brings the inevitable disgrace upon it and I inform you of the facts in full time for you to clear your skirts of the scandal by having him arrested, you wire me that my conduct is most extraordinary and that you will expect a full explanation from me. If you need any explanation of the reason why no reputable person who has any reputation to lose can stay with your paper for one moment under these circumstances, I shall not attempt to make it. There are some occasions when words are quite inadequate. This seems to be one of them.*
>
> *Faithfully yours,*
> *Winifred Bonfils*
> *Monday, April 25, 1904*

It seems Campbell was not the only one in Colorado or even in neighboring Western states to be duped by Silberberg—just a few days before showing up at Edwards's home, he had been seen with various mine and bank owners and even Governor William Clark of Montana and former governor Thomas from Colorado. Still, it was embarrassing, and Campbell had to scurry to not only get rid of Silberberg but to mollify Black and keep the *Post* from repeating the *Colorado Springs Gazette* story.

There were other problems with *Polly Pry*. It was hugely expensive to run, owing in part to the glossy and colorful covers, its length, and some of the very popular writers Campbell employed for special issues and columns. For example, on April 2, 1904, *Polly Pry* ran a "Prosperity Issue," which heralded the "indisputable and inevitable greatness of our state" and employed guest commentators such as labor philosopher Henry George Jr., sports columnist W. W. Naughton, and popular novelist Edgar Saltus. Campbell employed veteran columnist and editor Stanley Waterloo—at a "very large salary"—to run some of the day-to-day operations of *Polly Pry* and also to solicit investment in a Chicago version of the periodical. Campbell's staff came up with the idea of raising the number of subscribers by offering a full four-year college scholarship to the youths who sold the most subscriptions. "Pack up your trunks, girls! Hunt up your football suits, boys! That college competition is so busy you can fairly hear the telephone wires 'siz' at the very name 'competition.'" Dozens of boys and girls dutifully sold hundreds of pledges to the magazine over the next three months, but there was never any scholarship nor any prize whatsoever given, nor was there any explanation.[3]

Campbell was not above calling in favors from high-powered friends to subsidize *Polly Pry*. She wrote to millionaire Simon Guggenheim in March 1904, asking him for money in return for an interview in the "Prosperity" edition:

> *The frontispiece will have a picture of His Excellency, Governor Peabody, and in the personalities we will probably give mention, with photographs, of four leading men of the state. In a conversation which I have just had with Mr. Williams, your name was suggested as one of the four, and it was heartily approved by the Governor. Should you decide to go in on this, we will, if necessary, send a reporter of note to New York to interview you, thereby giving it considerable prominence. In regard to compensation, will say that the amount proposed by us to you, of a general subscription of $2500, will include in this any further assistance we can render you.[4]*

Guggenheim did not take Campbell up on her offer. And others, like E. B. Field, president of the Colorado Telephone Company, waited until the last possible minute to pay what they had promised.[5]

Polly Pry would always cover labor conflict in some way, shape, or form until the end of its run, but in late spring 1904, an event transpired that would effectively slow the Cripple Creek strike and strife for a few years. On June 6, there was an explosion at the Independence mine that killed several nonunion miners. The Citizens' Alliance brought in the National Guard, which on June 7 shot into the Western Federation of Miners (WFM) union hall. The Citizens' Alliance also set up kangaroo courts and convicted and deported nearly 240 miners who refused to renounce their union memberships. The Cripple Creek strike did not officially end until December 1907, and the WFM's struggle in Colorado helped inspire the creation of the even more radical Industrial Workers of the World (IWW) in 1905. But in the summer of 1904, Campbell began to fill her paper with more political observations, though often enough politics was entwined with that of labor forces.

As with many other states during this time, Colorado was in the midst of a reformation—people were concerned with changing social injustices, economic discriminations, and political corruption. More often than not, these areas were merged, for one of the most immediate concerns of the reformers was the alliance between entrenched economic interests and the political machinery of government. To many, it seemed the battle needed to be waged with political institutions and candidates because only when these had been cleaned and returned to the people for their own use could social and economic injustices be legislated away.[6]

Denver reformers concocted a scheme for action, beginning with a constitutional amendment to allow Denver the right to establish "home rule." Simply stated, municipal home rule is a form of self-government in which local citizens control the organization and operation of local government activities rather than state officials. This change would divorce local politics from the vortex of state affairs—in other words, the municipality could make its own local laws and run its own utilities without the need for state legislation. Ideally, this would give a city and possibly its county some relief from abusive national political machines, which often used growing cities as a way to offer "spoils" to supporters. For example, in the case of Denver, the governor of Colorado had until then used his power to appoint members of the fire and police boards—usually people who had experience at the state level but who had little or no knowledge of what the burgeoning city needed in terms of fire and police control.

Then in order to eliminate unnecessary expense and to simplify the government of the municipality, reformers proposed that the City of Denver and the County of Denver be merged into one body politic, with provision for annexation of other areas in the future. In 1904 they presented their plan to the voters, who approved the constitutional amendment in the first major victory for reformers, or as they soon called themselves, the "progressives."[7]

Campbell was adamantly against Denver's home rule and fought valiantly with her paper to sway citizens to vote against it. "Until the people of Denver actually show that they have finished with the spoils system," she said, "it would be the very height of asininity to build up any more political machines by creating any more appointive offices." She gave example after example, such as this one of Denver's highly praised tramway system:

Suppose the city of Denver had owned the street railway system— do you think we would have had our present magnificent Tramway system? Never in a thousand years. The horse car would never have been superseded by the cable, nor the cable by the electric. . . . So with the Water company: If any city owned it, do you think for a moment we would to-day have the vast and expensive system which has been built up at an enormous outlay of money, time and intelligence, under its present management? Never![8]

Campbell's underlying concern with home rule was that whoever took control of the transportation systems on a local scale would be able to control who registered to vote and who actually made it to the polls on the appropriate day. "The Tramway Company employs about 900 people. This would make places for a whole lot of the faithful, wouldn't it? And think of the opportunities afforded for proselytizing." The conductor, she continued, could give free fares to those who shared either his own political beliefs or those of the corporation that hired him in the first place and make sure they voted in lockstep when the occasion rose.[9]

Campbell's pontificating about politics in Denver and the West at large usually meandered into women's roles in it. In fact, in her tirades against home rule, she awkwardly swung her train conductor example to that of what happened with a female sanitary inspector. This woman, a Denver resident, was hired by a Democratic commissioner. When she kept reporting about the dirty and noisy affairs of a poorhouse in the center of town, she was called to "an inner room" and informed that the shack in question belonged to one of "our beloved county commissioners" and that she would lose her job if she kept making a fuss about it. Campbell also relayed stories like that of Alma Beswick, "not a bad-looking woman" but nonetheless not one who belonged to any bona fide women's clubs; Beswick remained on the payroll of Democrats who had her cart poorhouse residents to the home of any relatives she could find outside the city proper, thus allowing them to cut off welfare recipients in Denver.[10]

Still, Polly Pry recognized that Colorado occupied a unique place in the history of female suffrage and that its future rested on how women themselves perceived their role in politics. By the time *Polly Pry* came into existence in 1903, women in Colorado had had the right to vote in statewide elections for ten years. (Wyoming gave its female citizens the vote in 1869 but did not become a state until 1890.) Campbell frequently sought out commentary from national leaders of female suffrage, including that of her colleague Winifred Black and her relative by marriage Susan B. Anthony, who had very different viewpoints on the future of women and voting:

THE FEMININE FRAUDS IN POLITICS!

Susan B. Anthony

It is not expected that voting will change a woman from a devil to an angel. . . . The great good to my mind is that when a low-lived, ignorant, drunken, gambling, licentious man meets a woman he cannot feel that his opinion is to be counted at the ballot box, to regulate all the laws with regard to civil institutions, while her opinion means nothing. He must now feel that he meets his equal, at least, and her vote will be against his in the great majority of cases. . . . Has it [suffrage] lowered the moral tone of woman? No, not a particle more *than when a woman goes as a missionary to the heathen her morals are lowered to the status of the heathen. When a woman votes for the shutting up of the saloon, the gambling house and the brothel, she does not put herself below the man who votes in favor of all of them, but places herself above him.[11]*

Winifred Black

Women have been voting for the past eight years and haven't closed one tiny little bit of a saloon yet, to say nothing of the others mentioned in your statement—not one. Politics is the business of men, just as religion is the business of women, and as the husband rue-fully follows to church at his wife's heels, so the wife goes to the polls by husband's advice, and all the rights of franchises on earth won't alter the case—glory be to the Maker of us all, who created us just the same—only different.[12]

Campbell's commentaries about suffrage and her political activism in general attracted the attention of another female star in Colorado and national literary circles. Ellis Meredith, was, in 1904, already known as the "Susan B. Anthony of Colorado." Born in Bozeman, Montana, in 1865, she was the daughter of Emily R. Meredith, a well-known proponent of women's right to vote, a cause Ellis herself would take up. At twenty-four, Ellis Meredith had her own column called "Woman's World" in the *Rocky Mountain News*, an impressive feat for a woman of the day, particularly for someone so young. Her activist viewpoints and articles made her a political giant, as her friend and author Carlyle Channing "Cad" Davis, proclaimed: "Ellis Meredith is a name to conjure with. Physically but a midget, tipping the balance below a hundred pounds, she yet is one of the most influential and forceful characters ever connected with the press in the Centennial State. . . . Intellectually she is a prodigy. In her grasp of the fundamentals she is a wonder." Ellis focused on women's rights and the temperance movement to the exclusion of other social, economic, and polit-ical issues of the day, as her critics often pointed out. The *Denver Post* once referred to her as "somewhat insane." She wanted the complete removal of alcohol, not just a limited intake, because at the time many intoxicated men abused women and children. Ellis wanted an end to this and hoped for women to be treated equally and with respect.

Elected as the vice president of the Colorado Non-Partisan Equal Suffrage Association in 1890, Meredith continued to work for women's rights and temperance. She met Susan B. Anthony at the Chicago World's Fair in 1893, where she learned from Anthony how to create a strong connection between local activism and national activism, which strengthened the women's suffrage movement.

Meredith's campaigning and years of hard work helped secure Colorado women's right to vote in 1893. However, her place in politics did not end there. In 1903, Meredith was elected as delegate to the Denver City Charter Convention. She had to leave her job as an editor for the *Rocky Mountain News* for this new position. She also served on the Democratic Party State Central Committee and then as the city election commissioner. In 1904, she spoke in front of the US House of Representatives, calling for the national government to amend the Constitution to provide women's suffrage.

Nell, of course, was a staunch Republican while Meredith was an avowed Democrat. Locally, they were on opposite sides of Denver's home rule charter. Both women, however, considered themselves able to exert their political writings and pressure for candidates and issues that they believed would benefit humanity. "Whether it is owing to woman's suffrage or not," wrote one gentleman in *National Magazine*, "the women of Denver are more actively interested in public life and matters than in any other city in the Union. . . . Miss Ellis Meredith, vice-chairman of the Democratic State National Committee, is not only a brilliant writer and author, but is a thorough-going politician. . . . Mrs. Anthony, 'Polly Pry,' is also a resident of Denver, and I must confess that a Colorado experience would convince any normal man of the merits of woman's suffrage."[13] Campbell even gave a nod to female Democrats in *Polly Pry*, speaking of their organizing activities for the 1904 Colorado gubernatorial election: "If the Democratic women do this [organize], they will win out, because the brethren can't carry an election without them; and they wouldn't stand a ghost of a show for a look-in if they lose Denver. . . . I hope the Democratic women will go after this and go after it hard. They have never had a square deal, and they never will until they assert themselves a little bit."[14]

Nell and Ellis took opposite sides of one of Colorado's most notorious political scandals, which involved the 1904 gubernatorial election. Naturally, Campbell stumped for James Peabody while Meredith did the same for Democrat Alva Adams. The 1904 election was rife with fraud. The Democratic Party allegedly committed voting fraud in Denver and the surrounding urban areas. The Republican Party was said to have committed voting fraud in the populous mining and corporately dominated towns. In one Denver precinct, 717 Democratic ballots were cast, while the district had only one hundred legal voters. Likewise, many mine owners forced thousands of immigrant workers to vote for Governor James H. Peabody or lose their jobs. One Republican officer of the Denver Union Water Company publicly boasted, "We rule. . . . The people have nothing to do with nominations and elections. We rule and we're going to continue to rule." Despite these presumptions, Democrat Adams was elected governor, while Republican Jesse McDonald became lieutenant governor.

Once the legislature came into session in 1905, however, party fighting became so blatant that it risked making the Colorado General Assembly a laughingstock. After much argument and accusations of election fraud, the predominately Republican legislature agreed that neither Adams nor Peabody should be governor. Instead, Jesse Fuller McDonald took the oath, stepping up from his position as lieutenant governor. Peabody thus served as the thirteenth and fifteenth governor of Colorado, while Alva Adams served as the fifth, tenth, and fourteenth. Peabody assumed the office, named McDonald as his lieutenant governor and promptly communicated his resignation to the Colorado secretary of state, at which point McDonald became the sixteenth governor of Colorado. Colorado is the only state to have had three governors serve in a single day.

It was Ellis Meredith who supported Nell's ambitions to open a branch of *Polly Pry* in New York: "But this is to say to you that you are to go in good cheer," she wrote Campbell sometime in 1905, "I have faith in your New York plan and believe you are going to make a winning. No one ever puts up as long, hard, brave a fight as you without winning out in the end. You don't know it, not being overly bright in some ways, but you are one of the most remarkable, and one of the most gifted women in this country."[15]

Unfortunately, Nell's New York newspaper venture never came to pass. She filed articles of incorporation for an East Coast version of *Polly Pry* in August 1905, but financial troubles for her Denver flagship left her without enough capital to start something new. The next month, Campbell sold *Polly Pry*, her "baby," to William H. Griffith, who at one time had published the *Denver Times* and *Sun*, among other papers. Grudgingly, the *Telluride Journal* said goodbye to the paper whose owner had spent so much time reporting on the worst of its district during the mining wars of 1903 and 1904: "Whatever we may think of the late lamented *Polly Pry* magazine, it sparkled with brilliancy as compared with its successor, the *Saturday Sun*."[16]

The loss of her paper forced Campbell to face some stark realities. She had no income and no future employment prospects. It seems she did not have enough money to cover the rent of her Colfax Avenue home, so she set up lodgings at the swanky Brown Palace Hotel in Denver while she planned her future. According to various newspaper accounts, Campbell traveled quite a bit back and forth between Denver and New York for the next twelve months or so, trying to raise capital for a new newspaper—perhaps one out of New York itself.

The stress must have been palpable, for the few letters in Campbell's file at the Denver Public Library reflect her friends' concerns for her disposition. One, for example, counseled her on making nice with someone with whom she was either romantically involved with or with whom she was trying to forge a new business or both:

> *There is much I'd like to talk over with you Polly—so much you ought to know about & Polly—you must fix this quarrel up with Guy— you need his good will, dear—you really do, Polly—you must realize this—be good friends at any rate—at any cost, Polly—whether you resume business interests together or not. I fancy you will be displeased at receiving this but Polly, in justice to you and all your kindness to me in the past, I want you to be true to yourself—and you're not. You are*

your own worst enemy—May God give you all that I would give you
if I were God. Cause I love you.
        Gertrude[17]

Friend Ellis Meredith was also deeply concerned about Campbell, and perhaps had loaned her money:

My Dear Nell,
    There is no need to tell you that I am going to do my best for you, because I would do that in any event. I have done so for people I don't care a straw for, and who have been far less generous than you have been. I'm not saying it will be much of a best, because I don't know anything about this kind of thing, but, such as it is, I'll mean well.... But this is to say to you that you are to go [to New York] in good cheer, and not worry.[18]

Both of these letters discreetly referenced a matter that was kept out of the newspapers entirely, no small feat even for those entrenched in the newspaper business. This matter was the fact that Campbell was likely at this time very close—perhaps too close—to a married man, one whose divorce was about to explode across local headlines. This gentleman was Henry "Harry" J. O'Bryan, and Campbell's close friends knew she was tempting fate by being attached to him:

The world is brighter and happier for me & a lot of people because you are in it. Tell Harry he is to pray on the rosary for you, for himself, and for success, and that he is to be very good to you, or I will not lend him so long anymore. Well, dear, try to understand how more than dear you are to me, how anxious I am for your happiness—and that includes H's [Harry's]. I can't say what I want to, but maybe you will comprehend.[19]

Campbell's friend Gertrude offered similar allusions:

Polly dear—will you please say to Mr. O'B for me—that its sorry I am that he is playing to such hard luck—my heart just aches for him and the wife—the babies—its such a heartache for all concerned—I'm so truly—so sincerely sorry that things took the turn they did yesterday.[20]

Gertrude was referring to the press's discovery that the estranged wife of Campbell's close friend or lover Harry O'Bryan had returned to Denver from Paris in order to obtain a divorce.

O'Bryan was a very colorful figure in Denver society. Born in 1868 to a prominent Pennsylvania attorney and his society wife, Harry became a lawyer himself at the age of twenty-one. Also in 1889, he met and married Miss Mamie Otero, the sister of Miguel Otero, who later became governor of the territory of New Mexico. Their wedding, wrote the *Albuquerque Citizen*, "was one of the most brilliant social events pulled off in the territory."[21] The newlyweds moved to Denver in the early 1890s and quickly became society favorites. They had two children in quick succession, and O'Bryan's practice grew rapidly. Mamie O'Bryan was a petite but athletic woman, routinely taking trophies in golf and tennis, and was also very beautiful, described as being of "Spanish attraction, with black hair, very large, wide open blue eyes, and a glorious pink and white skin."[22] O'Bryan was often described as "debonaire," "handsome," and "poetic." He and Ellis Meredith were colleagues because of his work on behalf of the Democratic Party in Denver.

Nell and Harry almost certainly met when Harry Tammen and Frederick Bonfils were charged with jury tampering during the 1901 trial of the would-be attorney of alleged cannibal Packer, W. W. Anderson. O'Bryan was appointed prosecutor but initially demurred: the defendants asked for an immediate trial, and he thought it was peculiar that they would do this while claiming to be innocent. Harry, knowing full well how devious Tammen and Bonfils could be and suspecting something amiss, refused to try the case against them without having the time to dig further and get proper witness statements. "When I accepted the position it was with the understanding that there were to be no [time] restrictions to be placed upon me. I intend to probe the matter to the very bottom, so there will be no necessity for a grand jury investigation."[23]

Harry and Mamie's marriage appeared to crumble around 1902, as Harry's behavior started to become more and more erratic. In November of that year, Miss Maggie Horan sued O'Bryan for refusing to give back $3,800 of hers held in trust while she settled a different lawsuit. In August 1903, Colorado Springs stockbroker Peyton Randle had O'Bryan arrested for passing him a bad check in the amount of $15. Randle said he was anxious about the whole thing because he considered Mr. and Mrs. O'Bryan good friends and hated to bring notoriety to their names, but he could not get Harry to resolve it quietly.[24] In June 1905, a Denver judge ordered O'Bryan to appear in court for failure to pay $150 in back wages to his stenographer. And O'Bryan's drinking habit was a poorly kept secret: he was often referred to as the "cocktail-mixer" of Denver. His close friends had noticed some changes in him for a couple of years: "He told more stories and did even less work; the gin cocktails grew better and better; the clothes were not quite so good; vague rumors of vague misdoings followed him everywhere like a miasmic mist; he left his clubs, whether by invitation or not, no one exactly knew."[25] O'Bryan complained to the *Mountain News* that his temperament was not made for Mamie's "nagging habit" when he needed quiet and that he had been the victim of a "death blow" when his wife, "in a fit of 'malicious spite'" had sold his beloved pet dog.[26]

When Nell and Harry became romantically involved is not clear, but what is certain is that they were both in New York when the newspapers caught wind of O'Bryan's divorce. Mamie had quietly taken the children to Paris in 1902 and engaged an apartment next door to Mrs. Sarah O'Bryan, Harry's mother. The women returned to the United States to tend to a very ill sister of Harry's and while in New York City learned of Harry's presence there. Hoping for a quiet, uncontested proceeding, Mamie and her children hurriedly traveled west and filed a claim for divorce in Denver. Unfortunately, the press was finely attuned to the comings and goings of its citizens, especially one that had once been a fixture on its social scene. "She is terribly embarrassed at the notoriety given the affair in this morning's papers," said her sister-in-law Mrs. Grattan O'Bryan. "She had hoped it would be suppressed and the publicity is a great trial to her sensitive nature. Of course, there is nothing which can be told that is not already public property, but her position is indeed a most painful one. The nature of the complaint? Simply non-support; that was the most womanly position for her to take."[27] The papers wondered how O'Bryan was supporting himself in New York. "Some say he is writing for the magazines; others, that he is following the races; still others, that he is living as did the old Cigale in the old French song, simply, in the sunshine of the day that follows day."[28]

In truth, O'Bryan was living in New York City with Nell. It seems that despite his once-lucrative law practice, he had spent everything he had. "The big house on the hill went the way of all the Harry O'Bryan property long since," wrote one reporter, referring to his divorce from Mamie, "and it is said that book by book, the fine library melted away to pay for certain necessities in the way of liquid refreshments without which, it is whispered, life would be to Mr. Harry O'Bryan one long and Omarless desert."[29] How the pair generated an income for themselves isn't known. It seems Harry tried to begin a law practice in his new state of residence, but when the New York Bar Association wrote to Colorado's as part of his application process, it received a negative response because of so many complaints about O'Bryan's performance there. He was denied license to practice in the state of New York. And Campbell's financial problems dogged her as well: in October 1906, she and the new owner of *Polly Pry* were sued for more than $1,000 in overdue payments owed to vendors for the paper.[30]

Mamie and Harry's divorce was granted November 7, 1905, with Harry in absentia. Nell Ross Campbell Anthony and Harry J. O'Bryan were quietly married on August 2, 1906, in Hoboken, New Jersey.[31]

Chapter 11

Polly Pry and Pancho Villa, Part I

Polly Pry remained in New York with Harry for the next year and a half, except for a brief visit to Denver for her mother and father's golden wedding anniversary in January 1906. It is possible that Campbell went to considerable lengths to keep her marriage to Harry out of the newspapers not just to prevent any gossip of her as an adulteress but because she felt genuine sympathy toward the first Mrs. O'Bryan and the children. In fact, she may have even used her influence with Denver newspapers to frame Mamie in the most positive light possible. More than a year after the O'Bryans' divorce, the *Denver Post* was still publishing flattering commentary about her:

> *A rumor now and then from the other side of the Atlantic reminds us that we have many social favorites who have taken up residence on the European continent. Not that we need to have our memories jogged to realize they are not with us, for there are those in Denver society who can never be forgotten. First among these is Mrs. Mamie O'Bryan. . . . A rumor from over the sea says that Mrs. O'Bryan has been remarried. This, however, has been denied emphatically by her sister-in-law, Mrs. J. Grattan O'Bryan, who received a letter from her last week. But that Mrs. O'Bryan should have many suitors is easily understood by those who remember this charming, highly educated and exceedingly pretty woman. She was as great a social success as Denver has seen, and it is clearly to be seen how she would be admired and pronounced a beauty in Paris.[1]*

To be sure, the *Post*—along with virtually every other early twentieth-century newspaper—always needed content to fill its society pages.

But the fact that nothing was written about the coupling of Harry and Nell—both of whom were public figures—indicates that one or both of them went to some trouble to keep it out of public view and also to keep Mamie's reputation intact and perhaps even to open her up to new marriage candidates. Mamie did not ask for—and O'Bryan did not offer—any future or retroactive support for her or the children, so finding her a mate for financial reasons did not figure into any underhanded plan. "There are always two parties to every divorce case," Campbell once wrote in *Polly Pry*, "and there are more men [who] get divorces through fraud and deceit than there are women. When a woman gets to the place where she wants a divorce, she is generally rather anxious to have the world know that she is a free woman."[2]

Nell and Harry returned to Denver some time in 1908 without any fanfare. They rented rooms on Decatur Street in the Highland neighborhood, near the city's center. O'Bryan returned to practicing law. Campbell embarked on the playwriting career she had tried to launch as a younger woman in the 1890s. The result of this endeavor was *By Order of the President*.

Ironically, *By Order*—Campbell's first produced play—did not cast Theodore Roosevelt in a favorable light, a sharp reversal from just a few years prior when Campbell lauded him as the defender of the United States' "flag, its purity and honor" and told her readers that a vote for the colonel was a vote for "decency, honesty, courage and Colorado," along with many other platitudes about the twenty-sixth president of the United States.[3] "Polly Pry has the nerve to criticize very harshly the action of Roosevelt and Taft in the Brownsville matter in her play," wrote the *Denver Post* in June 1908, "and there is no telling what will happen to her after Teddy hears about it."[4]

The "Brownsville matter"—more formally known as the Brownsville Incident or the Brownsville Affair—was the result of incidents that began in July 1906. The First Battalion of the 25th United States Infantry Regiment was a black unit under the command of white officers. They were usually referred to as buffalo soldiers. After serving in the Philippines, the regiment was deployed to Fort Brown near Brownsville, Texas. The soldiers immediately confronted racial discrimination from local businesses and suffered several instances of physical abuse from federal customs collectors. They were refused service in bars, subjected to racial slurs, and assaulted in the street by residents.

Tensions rose to their highest level on August 13, 1906. The black soldiers were accused by local white citizens of murdering a bartender and shooting a police officer. The soldiers consistently denied taking part in the attack, and their white commanders asserted that the soldiers were in their barracks during the shooting. With no credible evidence and based only on white accusations, President Theodore Roosevelt ordered the discharge of 167 black infantrymen for refusing to admit to or implicate fellow soldiers in the shooting. Many of these men had given several years of service and missed earning their pensions as a result of the dismissal.

In what could only be called a brilliant piece of promotional material for her upcoming play, Campbell wrote a full-page article about her experience with the buffalo soldiers during her residence in Mexico. She recalled a dry, dusty afternoon from a "long, long time ago," when she and some unnamed companions had gone up to a lumber camp in Chihuahua to inspect some railroad ties. Campbell and her fellow travelers were ignorant of the fact, she wrote, that Apaches were in that part of the territory and were shocked when a cattleman told them to hurry down to the tiny fort nearby for safety because Geronimo was close and on the warpath. As day turned to night, and Campbell walked the roof with the lookout, her heart "fluttered like a frightened bird at every waving shadow on the desolate plain," and her blood froze at the frightful stories told of the "most inhuman devil who ever lived in this Western world."[5] Just as everyone was losing hope that they could be rescued, Campbell wrote, they saw a tiny dark speck on the horizon . . . and then another:

> *They came out of the desert just as the sun went down—soldiers—our soldiers! Ah! The blissful relief of that moment! When I reach the Great White Gate, I hope the sight I'll see will afford me one-half the joy that I felt when I looked upon that line of dusty black faces.*
>
> *Negroes?*
>
> *Yes, negroes: And brave and loyal soldiers, every one of them.*
>
> *They came fresh from a victorious fight with the Indians, scarred, maimed and deadly weary, but cheerfully indifferent—bringing in*

a wounded settler and his family, whom they had found fighting for their lives, their home on fire in a dozen places and surrounded by a horde of howling demons.

Campbell recalled how she felt about this regiment of soldiers when war with Spain broke out in 1898:

I felt a personal interest in their fate. And when the doughty colonel of the famous Rough Riders led his men into the ambush where poor Hamilton Fish was killed and the Rough Riders stood to be annihilated, and the Twenty-fifth came rolling like a black cloud to the rescue, I joined my shrill pipe to the general shout and added another page to my mental pictures of the gallant blacks.

Polly Pry then related the facts of the recent events and the emotional tug that led her to write her stage play:

In six weeks an unknown number of these soldiers—these tried and proved men with from eight to twenty-eight years of service behind them with the confidence of their officers and the respect and regard of the nation—these officers are charged with having wantonly and without provocation gone out of the fort and "shot up" the town. . . . In Washington, I saw the order for the "discharge without honor" of all that battalion. . . . The "colonel" had forgotten the Cuban hillside, but I remembered the gray dawn of a faraway morning, the tired eyes of a young officer and the smiling faces of a group of weary black men.

"Do you understand," Polly asked her readers, "why I wrote my play?"[6] In fact, they did. Many Americans were outraged at Roosevelt for his decision. Roosevelt had previously enjoyed good political support among African Americans. Roosevelt purposely withheld news of the discharge of the soldiers until after the 1906 congressional elections so that the pro-Republican black vote would not be affected. Many hoped that the judicious William Howard Taft would intervene, and Taft privately urged Roosevelt to reconsider but did not take a public stand against the decision for fear of adversely affecting his chance to be the next president.

The spunky journalist may have felt deeply about this incident on a personal level, even if she had never met a black soldier. That summer of 1908, Theodore Roosevelt was campaigning for a third term as president against William Jennings Bryan, a Democrat and one who vociferously criticized corporate power at the expense of the people. He was closely allied with the American Federation of Labor and, like the Democrats in general at that time, criticized the use of unfair tactics to stop workers from striking or penalize them if they did. In other words, Bryan represented almost everything Nell despised; promoting the inadequacies of Roosevelt would surely only help Bryan. It is difficult to know whether this was her intention or if she simply felt the Brownsville Incident was good drama—after all, Colorado and the other Western states had already overwhelmingly voted for Bryan as their candidate and would no doubt provide their votes again in the November 1908 election. A local play would hardly make a difference.

In any event, Denverites liked *By Order of the President*, and not just because it vilified Roosevelt. "It's a thriller, that play," the *Post* wrote, "I've read it, and speak from a fullness of gooseflesh knowledge. It goes with a zip and hurrah, accompanied by the most delicate and picturesque sentiment imaginable."[7] Of course, this reviewer happened to be Campbell's friend Pinky Wayne, but others praised her first production as "daring in conception," "dashing in action," and satisfying, if not overwhelming. Another *Post* review gave Campbell kudos for nabbing popular actor Theodore Lorch as part of the cast, though it pointed out the obvious, which was that there were no black actors in the play: "To be sure, the bleaching of the battalion dishonorably discharged from the service because of the Brownsville incident would seem to rob the play of an excuse for being, but the dramatic fires are kept a-burning by author and an acting white soldiery."[8] The newly minted playwright injected the real Brownsville events with a dramatic love story, where a beautiful and accomplished girl of a "Southern type" falls in love with a college man from Boston. There was one act that held a full one hundred actors on the stage, including a company of soldiers in full uniform.[9]

Encouraged by the full attendance of her one-week run at the Curtis Theater, Campbell began penning more plays. She and Ellis Meredith wrote several together, mostly Bible-inspired works and some based on society women, such as *A Modern Portia* and *An American Suffragette*. These were not financial windfalls, but Harry had returned to practicing law and presumably made a modest income, while Campbell earned some extra money as a freelance writer and editor for the Colorado state government.

The turn into her sixth decade of life was not terribly kind to Campbell. Her brother Charles, already disabled with various lung problems, was in a horrific train crash in August 1909, in which both of his legs were fractured. Her beloved father Nelson died on July 8, 1910. Less than eighteen months later, Charles passed away at age 55 as a result of complications from his injuries. Around the same time, her mother, Mary, fell ill with heart problems and had to begin taking in boarders to pay her bills.

The end of her second marriage may have triggered Campbell to reinvent herself once again. On January 27, 1914, Nell filed for divorce from Harry. Both the *Post* and the *Mountain News* reported it the next day: she charged "non-support, cruelty and drunkenness." The attorney had been missing for about two weeks when Campbell discovered that he had bigamously married Denverite Mrs. Eva Johnson Fredd in Portland, Oregon, ten days earlier. Campbell's feelings about the demise of her marriage are not recorded, but it had to have been greatly disappointing, especially since she was his companion throughout the scandalous end of his first union with Mamie. The divorce did not even have time to wend through the court; O'Bryan died of a heart attack on March 23, 1914, in his hotel room in Portland. He was forty-seven. This same day, Campbell applied for a passport to Mexico.[10]

"Now for the facts!" blared the *Mountain News* on April 17, 1914. "Polly Pry, just back from Mexico, will begin the inside story of that unhappy country in *The Times* tomorrow. Uncensored and unhampered by 'diplomacy.' Just the facts. . . . This brilliant woman, recognized by newspapermen and magazine editors the country over as a fearless investigator and picturesque writer, was sent to Mexico four weeks ago by *THE TIMES* to GET THE REAL INSIDE STORY of the revolution which has turned that rich, but unhappy, land into a veritable shambles." (Business tycoon John C. Shaffer of Chicago had purchased the *Mountain News* and the *Denver Republican* in 1913 and merged the latter with the *Denver Times*, so Campbell's exploits were promoted in both papers.)

The revolution the *Mountain News* was referring to was the Mexican Revolution, which began as a series of upheavals in the north of that country in 1910. Initially, it was a movement of middle-class protest against the long-standing dictatorship of Porfirio Diaz. Like many of Mexico's nineteenth-century rulers, Diaz was an army officer who had come to power by a coup. Unlike his predecessors, however, he established a stable political system, in which the formally representative Constitution of 1857 was bypassed; local political bosses controlled elections, political opposition, and public order; and a handful of powerful families monopolized economic and political power in the provinces.[11]

This whole political system was built with new money pumped into the country by foreign trade and investment, much of it by the United States. In addition to a spiderweb of railways spanning the country, such as those built by Campbell's ex-husband's family, there were mines, export crops, paved streets, electric lights, trams, and sewage systems. Although other Latin American countries were developing similarly, these investments had a unique impact on Mexico, resulting in a revolutionary outcome. The oligarchy benefited from its relationships with foreign capital. For example, Luis Terrazas, a butcher's son, used his position as governor of Chihuahua to move armed forces in and out of portions of the state, creating instability in prices and personally buying up land where prices had decreased by his own doing. He eventually dominated the northern state, acquiring huge cattle estates, mines, and industrial interests.[12]

Outside investment also bolstered Mexico's national government— by the turn of the twentieth century, its credit rating was the envy of Latin American countries. In 1910, when the aging Diaz hosted world representatives on the hundredth anniversary of its independence from Spain, it seemed that peace and prosperity were assured. This year, despite having announced that he would allow a return to democracy and not run for president for an eighth term, Diaz reversed himself and ran against the very popular Francisco Madero, a wealthy cotton grower who had founded his own political party. The dictator had Madero arrested shortly after the latter announced his candidacy, but Madero escaped from prison and published the Plan of San Luis de Potosí, which called for the destruction of Diaz's authoritarian rule through violent means.

By the time Polly Pry began writing her articles in April of 1914 about the revolution in Mexico, Diaz was living in exile in France, and Madero had been executed by counterrevolutionary forces. In power was the regime of General Victoriano Huerta, who was backed by the United States, business interests, and those who wished to return to the "old order" of rule by rich and powerful families. Before Madero was killed, he convinced a well-known bandit to lead the fight against Diaz's forces on behalf of the common citizens of Mexico. This bandit was thirty-three-year-old José Dorotea Arango Arámbula, better known as Francisco "Pancho" Villa.

Villa is unique among legendary heroes because of the manner in which his legend was made. For the first eighteen years of his extralegal career, notes historian Nancy Brandt, stories about him were disseminated only by traditional methods, like word-of-mouth accounts and poetry and ballads. But the hero-bandit, because he was born in the late 1870s, became the subject of new media technology that emerged when he was in his early forties: the typewriter, rudimentary telephones, the linotype, the Kodak camera, wireless telegraphy, radio, even the first motion pictures made by Thomas Edison. Before he died, all of these inventions were used to propagate his legend.[13]

On April 18, 1914, the *Indianapolis Star* promised to give an "uncensored, uncolored account" of conditions in Juarez, Chihuahua, Torreón, and elsewhere by a "daring woman writer" who was with Villa's forces at the fall of Torreón. Like some other Western newspapers, the *Star* purchased the series of articles provided by the *Denver Times* and the *Rocky Mountain News* about Pry's exploits in Mexico. "It is a pathetic story," warned the *Star*, "a story almost beyond belief in many of its phases. Here you will see the true Villa, the merciless bandit, laying waste cities and plantations, plundering and despoiling, for the cause of—what?" The daily promised Polly's articles would shed light on the "blood-stained stage" of the drama of Mexico's destiny.[14] Ironically, Campbell's travels south meant that she could not report on the Ludlow Massacre, which occurred in Las Animas County on April 14, 1914, the deadliest single incident in the Colorado Coalfield War, which involved the Rockefeller family interests and strikebreakers from Mexico.

It is impossible to know whether Campbell ever met Pancho Villa or even went to Mexico. There is no reason to doubt she at least tried. She applied for and received a passport to travel south of the US border (she wrote "1869" as her birth year instead of "1859" on the application). The journalist may have forgotten some of the Spanish she learned while in northern Mexico with George Anthony decades before, but she certainly would have been able to get by with some familiar words and phrases. In 1913 and 1914, Villa welcomed newspaper correspondents, fitted up baggage cars as offices and living quarters for them, and saw to it that these correspondents' cars moved with his troop trains.

But as with her European adventures in 1901, Campbell likely never met the people she wrote about south of the American border, nor experienced most of the impossibly breathtaking adventures that were printed in the *Denver Times*. It does, however, seem probable that she traveled to El Paso, Texas, where many other journalists converged. She likely went to a few spots in Chihuahua that were familiar to her from living there two decades before. Among the many items in Campbell's possession at the time of her death is a telegram from an Alberto Pico, the grand general secretary of Masons in Mexico, who notified an intermediary that Campbell would have access to interviewees once she arrived in Mexico:

The Sovereign Grand Commander, to whom I referred your much appreciated letter dated March 24th, relative to the presentation of Mrs. Leonel Ross Anthony O'Bryan, has instructed (arranged by agreement) that I should reply to you, as I take pleasure in doing, that the said Mrs. Leonel Ross Anthony will be very well received and presented to all those persons whom she may deem necessary.[15]

The level of detail woven into her dispatches from Mexico shows that Campbell had at least some information that was not readily available to the general public, which supports the idea that she spent some time in the company of those who were receiving firsthand reports, probably in El Paso. An undated letter from Campbell's brother, Roy, urges her to take good care of herself while in El Paso. But it is ludicrous to believe that at age fifty-five, Nell Campbell—or anyone else, for that matter—could bob and weave around hundreds of miles of war-torn Mexico without serious difficulties—more difficulties than the mere hassles she wrote about in her dispatches. Additionally, there is a handwritten note on the Masonic telegram from George W. Vallery, a railroad magnate friend of Campbell's, who might have been displeased that he went through the trouble to get her safe passage in Mexico only for her not to use the favor to its fullest extent: "Dear Polly, Please note. I suppose you did not get as far south as Mexico City." Still, Vallery acknowledged that he enjoyed the fruit of her labors, calling her articles "bully," an adjective of commendation popularized by President Theodore Roosevelt. Polly Pry's own employer, the *Denver Times*, did not give exact dates for when she left and returned to Denver. But even a month was not enough time to travel down to the border from Denver and stop at all the places she purportedly visited.

Campbell, like every other reporter in the United States at that time, must have been well versed with the experiences of John "Jack" Reed, the twenty-six-year-old Harvard graduate and aspiring journalist whose desire for adventure outweighed his fear of death. Villa had won two major military victories against Mexico's military leader General Victoriano Huerta in late 1913. But US journalists—barred by the military from entering Mexico and deathly afraid of what might happen to "gringo reporters" in a land of machetes and machine guns—covered the war from the sidelines, submitting their copy on the larger-than-life Villa and his horseback army from the border town of Presidio. Frustrated, Reed requested an interview with the Mexican general in charge of the town of Ojinaga, across the border. "If you set foot in Ojinaga," the reply to Reed stated, "I will stand you sideways against a wall, and with my own hand take great pleasure in shooting furrows in your back." Reed decided to throw caution to the wind, crossed the Rio Grande, and walked into Ojinaga with his photographer Robert Dorman. By Christmas Day, Reed and Dorman were in Chihuahua City, Pancho Villa's headquarters, watching the man in person as his jubilant followers serenaded him with chants of "Viva Villa."[16] Reed's dispatches to the *New York World* from Mexico later that year made him the highest-paid journalist in the United States and opened the floodgates to dozens if not hundreds more journalists and photographers—a few of them women—who poured into northern Mexico around the same time as Polly Pry. Certainly, Campbell hoped to emulate Reed's financial success covering a region that used to be her home, and also to find excitement again—away from the society columns of Denver.

News coverage of the Revolution usually profiled Villa in one of two ways. The first way painted the rebel as someone to be greatly admired—a man very different from the purely selfish and utterly ignorant cutthroat and robber as he was often portrayed. For instance, *McClure's* magazine carried an article that compared Huerta and Villa, claiming that "Huerta could never rise to heights. Villa could." One syndicated newspaper article said that Villa's photograph showed "a man of considerable humor and great strength of character," while another opined that "it was conceivable that he had not been correctly painted by his enemies—those interested in continuing despotism in Mexico, with its concomitants of graft for the friends of the despot." The "leader," it said, only wished to make things right for the common man in his country, so he could go home and raise cattle in peace. The second way Villa was usually profiled was as a vicious bandit. One magazine depicted his life as "a recital of cold-blooded murders, thefts, torturings, and atrocities of an even worse description." Many portrayed him as a leader who forced compliance from his followers by fear, a coward who had groveled at Huerta's feet and begged not to be sent to the firing squad . . . a guerilla leader who paraded eighteen thousand soldiers at Aguas–calientes to insure that the convention would see things his way.[17]

Polly Pry took both approaches. She wrote both flattering and critical pieces about Villa, as she also did with Huerta, Madero, Madero's then-lieutenant Venustiano Carranza (Garza), and many other agents of change in the Mexican Revolution. Additionally, she wrote of the innocent men, women, and children and ravaged landscapes caught in the middle of Mexico's bloody transition between a dictatorship and a constitutional republic. What she wrote from April through June 1914 was enough to fill a book.

CHAPTER 12

Polly Pry and Pancho Villa, Part II

The man with the tanned face and gray eyes asked her: "Do you mind taking a little ride with me?"

"Delighted!"

Polly Pry hopped into the carriage with an American who had business interests in Torreón, Mexico. In a few minutes, they were rattling along behind two starved and emaciated horses that had huge raw sores on their backs, into which the "human brute" who drove them flicked his whip every few seconds. Unable to endure it any longer, Pry insisted she walk. The American listened to her indignant protest and joined her walking while the driver drove away, grinning and still beating his half dead animals. They walked past the electric light and power plant, "to where the land slopes towards the great dry river," at which point Polly's companion pointed to a low adobe building and told her a chilling story about his experience there three days prior:

I was in that corner room talking with the man I came to see when we heard a noise and looked out that side window. Down below, where you see that ridge, there was a shallow trench, and standing on the other side of it was a group of soldiers, some thirty or forty, an officer and a bugler, with a lot of yellow tassels hanging from his sleeve. Directly a column of men came into view beyond the end of that wall (pointing to a long mud wall just beyond us) the men in the center had their hands tied behind them and stumbled as they walked, and were prodded by the rifles of those on the outside. They stopped by that wall and groups of twelve of the bound men were taken down there, some fell down and had to be lifted up, and were kicked and beaten. Then the officer waved his hand, the bugle sounded, there was a crashing volley; before the smoke rolled away, another, and another line was thrust into position with ferocious brutality; then we saw the armed soldiers heave the still breathing bodies into the trench and shovel the sand in on them, stamping it down with their sandaled feet and pounding it with the butts of their rifles—laughing and talking.

Campbell looked at her companion. His leathered face was pale, and his eye "had the glint of steel when the sun strikes it."

"Yes," he answered in response to her unasked question, "they were volunteers, all right. No, I haven't been telling it promiscuously. You see, my life wouldn't be worth that," snapping his fingers, "if they knew that I had seen it, but I'm telling you because you seemed so cock-sure that all the rumors you had heard were exaggerations. I tell you, madam, you couldn't exaggerate anything that has been done here."[1]

Polly Pry took this man's advice and did not leave any detail out of her accounts of the massive conflict south of the American border. Campbell stoked the fears of readers who worried about complete lawlessness creeping over the border into the United States and the US government's perceived inability to more quickly force a stable regime: "We are proud to think that we are a great and powerful nation, but under our present 'watching and waiting' policy I saw American citizens daily humiliated by this tenth-rate power. Our American consuls' acts made impotent and abortive, and our position in this supposedly friendly country grown intolerable."[2]

According to her first missive about her quest to find Pancho Villa, Campbell took a room at the Paseo del Norte hotel in El Paso, Texas, before heading to Chihuahua. This piece, which ran in the *Denver Times* on April 20, 1914, carried all the trademarks of Polly Pry. She provided readers with context:

The interests, all the big interests, the oil companies, the smelters, the vast lumber companies, the multimillionaire land owners, the big mine owners and the Mexican capitalists who have fled before the storm—which their greed and avarice have helped to raise—are there. They fill the lobby and have suites of rooms above [me], where the *merry little game of bribery and barter goes blithely forward. . . . It is claimed that the Waters-Pierce and the Standard Oil companies have combined with the smelter interests and have pledged themselves to raise a sum of $50,000,000 gold, which has already been contracted for, and which is to go to General Carranza and General Villa the day that sees Villa in possession of all the country he holds today, together with Saltillo and Monterey.[3]*

She wrote of the dangers a traveler to Mexico faced at this time:

Today you cross the Rio Grande between armed guards, you walk between lines of sullen soldiers, you approach an official across the intervening barrel of a rifle, you only move with a military pass in your hand, you ride, if you are permitted to ride at all, over a hastily constructed railway which has taken place of the costly road which was ruthlessly destroyed three years ago during the Madero revolution . . . and which gives you no guarantee that you will ever reach your destination.

Polly Pry provided stereotypical profiles and sweeping generalizations about key players in the conflict, giving her readers the impression that she was able to get to lesser-known, root causes of conflict:

The chief of the Constitutionalists' trusted agents is Felix Summerfeld, a German Jew, with the wily sycophancy of an old clothes dealer and the farseeing vision of his race, where money is concerned. He came as a typical Chevalier d'Industrie into Chihuahua four years ago and, by his chance employment by an Associated Press man, came into contact with Madero, in whose cause he saw not only a rich meal ticket, but a stepping stone to the fortune he sought.[4]

She cautioned readers that they could not trust sources like Mr. Summerfeld, and therefore, she would not interview someone like him. She also established herself as someone who could get trusted, if unnamed, sources:

There is one thing, however—any person in search of truth does well to steer clear of this peculiarly well-informed individual. Also, it is an excellent plan to treasure up all the tales you hear in the Paso del Norte, if only for the pleasure of finding out their entire falsity when you get across the border.

However, I heard one story from an absolutely disinterested but well-informed man that not only bore all the earmarks of truth on its face but had so many corroborative symptoms in its favor that without positive proof I still believe it to be true—not the least strong factor in that belief being the frantic earnestness and stern disfavor with which it was denied by the various interested factions.[5]

And of course, Polly Pry often described the most well-known actor on the stage of the Mexican Revolution:

Civilization lies helpless and bound beneath the upward rush of this undreamed-of ferocity, above which towers the threatening figure of Gen. Francisco Villa, ex-convict, murderer and thief. A Geronimo of cruelty, a soldier of parts, a leader of men, a man to fear, who in three short years has by sheer brute courage and audacity stepped from the position of a hunted outlaw, a bandit chief, with a following of two dozen men, into the supreme command of more than 20,000 soldiers and the complete control of a full third of the country. Francisco "Pancho" Villa, illiterate, ignorant, arrogant, bloodthirsty and cruel, but a man who laughs at death, who knows no fear, who meets you with narrowed eyes of hatred and wide smile of friendliness, and must be reckoned with before peace is even thought of in this land.[6]

In the days following her alleged arrival at the Texas–Mexico border, 1914, Polly Pry painted scenes of desolation caused by the fall of Torreón, one of the most important and wealthiest cities in Mexico and one that contained the hub of railway communications in the north. Villa took control of Torreón on April 2, after which Polly saw him many times, "dashing about on horseback, accompanied by two or three officers," and clad in an old gray suit with his hat rolled back to show his "thick, black stubble of beard." Polly obtained a pass from one of Villa's generals who allowed her to visit hospitals and see the surviving, wounded Federal soldiers who'd fought against Villa's rebel forces. The sights here made Polly Pry "sick with horror":

They had been carried into the building, these wounded men, and left without other medical attention than that which could be given by two men and a woman nurse. Some of them had lain there eleven days, watching their comrades die and be eaten alive with flies and vermin. The nurses soon had exhausted their meager resources and were reduced to efforts to comfort the last hours of the dying and fruitless struggles to get rid of the unspeakable filth, even the thought of which shocks the mind. There was no water in the place, except what could be brought at risk of life from a tainted well in the next block—water that stank with corruption. Men died and were thrust into the street to lie rotting in the sun, or were covered with blankets and pushed into a corner to further pollute the air of that inferno.[7]

A few months later, in June of 1914, journalist Jack Reed would deliver a famous indictment of US involvement in the Mexican Revolution, noting that unlike the exciting and noble conflict portrayed in films (directed by and starring Villa himself, by way of the United States' Super Eight Film Company), most people had no idea what they were fighting for and did not relish revolution as a way of living. Reed argued that other journalists who traveled through the country would have a far different view of Mexico and its people than the gallantry and excitement portrayed in the films: "You will make the astonishing discovery that the peons are sick of war—that, curiously enough, they do not enjoy starvation, thirst, cold, nakedness, and wounds without pay for three years steady; that loss of their homes and years of ignorance as to whether their women and children are alive, does not appeal to them much."[8] Polly Pry already knew this and drew upon all of her previous reporting experience to show her readers the plight of common men and women caught in the crossfire of war. For example, there was Nurse Dorothea de la Cruz, who had refused to desert her charges when the order came to evacuate:

I'll not trouble your souls with a description of that place, nor what this wonderful woman had endured for the eleven days she had worked among the wounded, the dying and the dead; worked without rest or respite, until her fresh and beautiful face grew ashen gray and old, her glossy black hair was streaked with silver and in her great brown eyes you saw something that brought the hot tears to your own.[9]

There was the plight of Villa's commander Che-Che Campos, whose loved ones were killed by a Yaqui named Urbina:

They found his uncle beaten to death in the little home where Che-Che had been treated as a son, and the two pretty cousins gone. Later, down near the creek, in a bit of cleared space, they found the elder one, literally torn to pieces. The younger has never been heard from since, nor seven other young girls who were taken away that morning.[10]

And there were the displaced families of Amecameca, near Mexico City, who had traveled all the way to Fort Bliss in Texas to escape the ravages of war:

Their prize possessions, however, were hairless dogs, clad in gorgeous flannel wrappings, which they carried all that long way, while the two children of 5 and 7 walked, clad only in their black hair and wonderful endurance. They came when we stopped to look at the dogs and leaned confidently against the stately general, looking up at him with beautiful eyes, their smiling red lips showing flawless rows of pearly teeth while he patted their shining tresses and playfully tweaked their ears—at which they giggled delightedly.[11]

And in case anyone at home had forgotten, Polly Pry reminded them of the horrific train crash from almost two months prior on February 21, 1914, when Villa's rebels had placed a bomb on the track near an important hub in Lima, killing all fifty-five infantrymen and the British engineer on board. Polly's version was slightly different. The fifty-five passengers who died consisted of men, women, and children; the engineer escaped from the train and heroically tried to reach a station down the track where he could warn workers to wire the next passenger train:

With burning eyeballs and bursting lungs he got his engine uncoupled and in a moment was blindly running for his life, the big engine swaying madly as, the throttle wide open, he plunged from the tunnel in a rolling cloud of smoke to see, as in a lightning flash, the rail torn from the track, and flung himself with his last remnant of strength from the cab.

When he came to he found himself lying in a deep gully, bruised and battered, but no bones broken. He crawled up to the track and looked toward the tunnel, out of which shot a vast volume of thick smoke tinged with lurid light and myriads of sparks, looked at his watch and began to tremble—the train was due. The heat, even where he stood, was appalling, but he lay down with his ear to the rail, listening. All he heard was the roar of a mighty wind. Then he rose and started away. It was two days later that someone found him far down the mountain side, his ear pressed to the earth—listening. It was ten days before he was able to tell his story. The engine was found at the foot of the mountain. The fireman has never been seen since.[12]

Not all of the war was gruesome though, Polly told her readers. One night, walking back to her hotel, she and her companion found themselves outside the luxurious home of a "rich refugee" and were invited in by a young officer. A ball was in progress, and the officer twirled around "an ugly little Indian girl, who danced like a bear," while he sweated profusely. Tallow candles dripped and sputtered in place of electric lights that had been destroyed by vandals, and the pulsing music of a string orchestra throbbed through the lofty salon. Lace curtains, glittering mirrors with gold frames, marble statues, gilt chairs, and silken couches made a "curious setting" for the "weird mob" of soldiers and girls who whirled about. Here and there, khaki-clad officers danced with "awkward but pretty little brown creatures," decked out in the French finery of the banished Spanish señoritas. Naturally, Polly was asked to join in, so she shed her coat and danced with a young lieutenant from the south, while her unnamed companion danced with the "ugly little Indian girl." Despite the revelers' insistence that Polly remain, she and her friend sneaked out; the journalist left her youthful dance partner "with the soulful eyes" holding a rose that she had picked on the way in.[13]

Polly's articles were largely set against the backdrop of the Tampico Affair. On April 9, 1914, officials in the port of Tampico, Tamaulipas, arrested a group of US sailors—including, crucially, at least one taken from on board a ship's boat flying the US flag, and thus from US territory. Mexico's failure to apologize in the terms demanded by American president Woodrow Wilson led to the US Navy's bombardment of the port of Veracruz and the occupation of that city for seven months. Tensions ran high between Mexico and the United States, neither of which had joined the Great War yet but were looking at the rest of the world in alarm, as alliances were struck and both wondered about invasions from above or below. Among many other things, the US government feared Huerta's dictatorship would court a Japanese alliance, owing to the fact that Japan sent arms to his regime. Additionally, the United States feared Japanese immigrants in northern Mexico would join Huerta's forces and possibly help the dictator ally with Germany and take up arms against the United States. Polly advised her readers that a Japanese invasion could happen at any time, even if this was not quite an imminent threat:

America's naval officers, railway men, steamship officials, travelers and businessmen in Mexico all unite in the chorus of alarm over the growing volume of Asiatics in that country and its inevitable meaning . . . to the United States. We may ignore Japan and laugh at the "yellow peril" as long as the Japanese remain thousands of miles across the sea, but with the mustard-colored gentry gathering along 1,500 miles of our border within stepping distance of our homes, it becomes another question.[14]

The columns and columns of ink Campbell printed the first few days of her Mexico sojourn were meant to whet readers' appetites for her centerpiece story: Polly Pry would meet with the fighting man of the

Constitutionalist Army himself, Francisco "Pancho" Villa! She brilliantly laid a foundation for the contrasting descriptions Americans had come to expect with regard to Villa: trustworthy, ruthless, romancer, womanizer, benefactor of the poor, vicious murderer. But first she described the inner sanctum of the already near-mythological Pancho Villa, then calmly depicted her interview setting and set the scene for readers:

> *Having assured [Villa's guard] that I had no other object in life except waiting for General Villa, he showed me into a large room, where a long table was set for luncheon, and left me to myself. . . . Then for a long time everything was very quiet. I got up and walked about, stopping beside the table where some one had set up a huge water pitcher filled with roses and bugambiya [sic] flowers, tightly jammed together. I took them out of the pitcher, found a couple of glasses and amused myself arranging the flowers, filling the pitcher with the bugambiyas, trailing the gorgeous vines across the cloth and placing a glass of roses at either end of the table. I had just stepped back to view the effect when a harsh voice at my back said: "Bien, senorita. Esta muy bonita!"*[15]

Polly Pry's description of this known killer who was complementing her flower arrangement was especially verbose and detailed, surpassing even her own high bar for characterization:

> *I had thought him taller, not over 5 feet 9 or 10 inches, and stockily built, with the thick shoulders of an athlete and the bull neck of a prize fighter. His hands are the hands of a horseman; they are sinewy and strong and hairy but well shaped and not large. His feet are small, and his legs slightly bowed. His head is extraordinary. It is not exactly deformed, but it gives you an impression of something more misshapen than it really is, due perhaps to the fact that his huge jaw, broad face and high forehead, recedes into a queer domelike crown and flat back head, which even his crisp, curling thatch of jetty hair cannot round out to normal proportions. His cheek bones are high, his wide mouth, coarse and sensual, is filled with strong yellow teeth, which his*

short upper lip leaves perpetually bared. His nose is thick, short, a bit tip-tilted and pugnacious to a degree, but it is his eyes that are truly remarkable. They are large and well shaped, dark and luminous, eyes which should be beautiful if they were not so terrible. Once, I saw a coiled adder in the desert, its head reared to spring. I remembered it as our eyes met and clashed, and some way I felt a little cold, as if a drop of ice water had fallen on my naked heart.[16]

Polly Pry made this appraisal of Villa in "the flicker of an eyelash," and she supposed he did the same of her. He told her he thought her very brave to come down to Mexico at such a time; Polly Pry discounted her bravery and got her pen and paper ready:

"Are you not afraid?" Villa asked.
"No, general, why should I be?" Polly responded.
"Have they not told you that 'Pancho' Villa is a bandit?"
he demanded.
"Yes, but what of that? I've seen bandits before, and they
were only men."
"Where about?"
"In the penitentiary—and also Mexico."

This last response from Polly Pry made Villa's teeth come together with a "click" and thrust his jaw forward "rudely" as he snapped, "I suppose you know that I was three years in the penitentiary?"

The intrepid journalist certainly did know this and elicited the information she wanted her readers to have. "'Oh yes,' I answered cheerfully. 'I have heard that, along with many other things, but I was not thinking of you. I was remembering the bandit who used to terrorize the people up in your country twenty years ago. His name was Jim Blake, and he was a half-breed from Texas.'"

This breezy remembrance on Polly's part not only checked Villa's arrogance but seemed to endear her to him: "I remember him. He was killed when I was a boy, up in the Yaqui country, but he was no bandit; he was a fool... And you know my country?" She did, telling him about racing her horse against Tarahumara peoples and losing several times.

Polly Pry and the revolutionary had established a mutual respect, and Villa felt comfortable speaking with her now. He listened to Polly's "staggering Spanish" and "laughed uproariously at inconsequential things." He talked to her as "simple, elemental men talk when they are at ease." He reminded her that he was a common man who had learned to read and write in prison and that he had been an outlaw with a price on his head for fifteen years. He had fought for his friend Francisco Madero, and he would continue to avenge Madero's death and take money back from the Spaniards and Científicos, the thieves who took it from the people! And despite the fact that the veins on Villa's temples throbbed with anger as he spoke of the Spaniards, and his voice was harsh and savage, Polly pointed out some tough truths, reminding the revolutionary that hundreds of Spaniards had been born and raised in Mexico—that it was their home. "Is a rattlesnake a prairie dog because he lives in the same hole?" Villa retorted.[17]

Toward the end of the interview, Polly Pry asked Villa her most provocative question: was it true that he was to be financed by the oil companies in case he took San Pedro, Saltillo, and Monterrey? According to her story, his face flushed, and his eyes almost popped from his head in a rage as he thundered, "You Americans are crazy to meddle in things which do not concern you. . . . The day may yet come when I shall have to fight all foreigners!" Polly offered her hand and coyly asked, "But not an American woman who has come all this way to see you." He shouted, "Never!" and invited her to come see him again. She went back to her hotel, where she stood a long time staring out the window at the Cerrode [de] la Cruz, "on which a tall cross stretches its arms to heaven—a mute symbol of man's inhumanity to man," and for many hours, she told readers, she was haunted by the memory of a coiled adder in the desert.[18]

The last of Polly Pry's first batch of articles about the revolution appeared on April 30, 1914. A New York paper printed that they enjoyed the articles, but that enjoyment came with a caveat: "This is what 'gets' the *Enquirer*," wrote the paper on May 2, "Polly Pry carries the tale of what she saw all the way from El Paso to Torreon, yet she saw nothing that scared her off the job and experienced nothing that gave her pause for personal complaint. Doesn't that 'get' you, too?"

Despite the fact that Nell Campbell's whereabouts were not positively known when she tangled wits with "Mexican Robin Hood" Pancho Villa and many other figures involved with Mexico's fight for democracy, her articles were so popular that the *Denver Times* commissioned a sequel batch of stories about ongoing developments in that country. On July 17, 1914, in the *Indianapolis Star*, sister paper to the *Times*, Polly Pry told her readers of the lengths she went to in order to provide them with more information about the revolution in Mexico:

> *For six weeks I have been traveling by steamer and boat and yacht, by train and motor car, carriage and cart about the Pacific slope down in hostile Mexico. I spent two days at Magdalena Bay among 5,000 busy Japanese fishermen, who looked at me askance and bristled with animosity at my approach, while I vowed that if heaven forgave me I would never again come within 500 miles of a dead fish.*

She told of the sixty hours she crouched in the stern of a gasoline yacht, which "danced like a cockleshell across the mighty swells of the Pacific," and how she spent a week in the besieged city of Mazatlán, listening to the Mauser bullets zip and zing. She heard the crashing roar of cannon and starving people weeping before the governor's doors, and needy women and children assault the Chinese storekeepers there and loot their shops.[19]

A lot had happened on the world stage between the time Polly Pry "returned" to Denver in late April 1914 and the time she wrote of her travails getting to Mazatlán in July of the same year. On June 28, 1914, a Serbian nationalist assassinated the archduke and heir to the throne of Austria-Hungary, Franz Ferdinand. Before long, Austria and Serbia drew one European country after another into war. Meanwhile, in Mexico, rebel armies were unable or unwilling to conclude an agreement, and in the coming months, war for power erupted between Constitutionalist Venustiano Carranza and Villa. President Wilson took a "wait and see" position, hoping that Carranza would successfully consolidate his power and Villa would formally pledge his allegiance to him. In July, rebels captured Mazatlán, where residents had starved while forces fought over control of this port city. On July 14, 1914, dictator Huerta left Mexico to live in exile in Spain, increasing the amount of speculation about who would fill the power vacuum he left behind. These events served as the backdrop against which Polly Pry wrote her second series of articles about ongoing strife in Mexico.

The threat of Japanese collusion with Mexico against the United States was still a daily topic on news outlets across the United States. Polly underscored this fear by relating the utterances of Mexican citizens working on her ship bound for Mazatlán, who told her the Japanese were especially good sailors and could swarm the beaches of Mazatlán at virtually a moment's notice:

> *"Japanese," said the captain in response to [this] question, "why, yes, there's a lot of them in Lower California, and more on the mainland. They're hard workers and attend to their own business, but I'm sorry to see so many of them getting in so close to home. Fact is, while they're all right—ain't got a word to say ag'in them—they don't somehow jibe with our ideas and folks.*
>
> *"There's a lot of 'em at LaPaz, more at Guyamas and Hermosilla and scattered along the coast.*
>
> *"Oh, I should say there was somewheres near 30,000 of them— maybe more. Sturdy men, handy with shootin' irons; hard workers and a mighty silent lot."[20]*

One Señor Don Ramon, the customs agent, was not as polite with his descriptions of Japanese fishermen. As Polly was occasionally wont to do, she portrayed herself as a disinterested source and let an interviewee verbalize more base, if prevalent, stereotypical points of view—often while she was stereotyping the interviewee:

> *These were pigs. All they cared for was to fish and fish and to eat, and for play, to amuse, if you please, they pretended to be soldiers and drilled. Yes, almost every night, out there where the yellow sand lay packed into a hard, flat floor. It was tiresome to [this] gentleman of soul, who sighed for the song and the dance. No, there were no cock fights! Alas, no, there were also no bullfights! It was just as he had said—nothing!*

Just work, eat, work. He was, thank God, not a Japanese and had already sent in his resignation. He could not live among such people.[21]

"DEATH HORROR HOVERS OVER ALL MAZATLAN," screamed a *Denver Times* headline on July 22, 1914. After supposedly arriving there, Polly Pry described the abominable suffering in this Pacific shoreline city, wrought by four years of revolutionary fighting:

Whole streets where the better houses cluster are bare and deserted, the windows and doors boarded up and securely fastened. Every bank in the city is closed, except a little local concern that handles the worthless paper of the day. The big stores have been "closed pending stock-taking" for months, and those that remain open have almost bare shelves, and with one accord refuse all money except Federal bank bills, which only the rich possess.

Campbell reported of military officers eating and drinking plentifully at the Central Hotel, while an impoverished crowd gathered outside and stared at the food they could only dream about. One "poor wretch," naked save for a pair of cotton trousers, gazed especially hard, tears streaming down his gaunt face:

He had just come from the silent Pantheon where, in a hole scooped out by his own hands, he had laid his little uncoffined child, whose tiny, emaciated face was watered with his tears; he wrapped it in his old shirt, which was the only burial robe he could find; at home his woman, the girl he loved, waited his coming, her face to the wall, too weak from hunger to stand longer upon her feet.

Soon, Polly wrote, the man began to mutter and turned to leave, but before anyone knew what was happening, he rushed into the banquet room with a knife. Before he could attack the heartless officers, though, the pitiful man was overtaken by the smell of the meat and flung his weapon away to scoop up the food. He was immediately shot in the naked breast and, forgotten by everyone, his wife at home starved to death.[22]

The dauntless writer was often more than just a passive observer in her stories of war-torn Mexico. She was often caught in a train car or some kind of lean-to shelter when rebels and Constitutionalists began firing at each other and afterward would stoically put aside any fear so she could write about her ordeal. On more than one occasion, hostilities ceased because one general or another that Polly had befriended asked for a truce so that she might pass from the Constitutionalist lines to the rebel lines and back again and write of the plight of all involved in the conflict.[23]

Polly Pry supplied the *Denver Times* with twelve "new" articles about Mexico for its July editions of the paper, all drenched with stories of despair, violence, and ruin, with equal parts hope, calm, and beauty, plus plenty of adventure thrown in for good measure. In total—when added to her April work—she had written about sixty thousand words about Porfirio Diaz, Pancho Villa, Francisco Madero, Venustiano Carranza, Victoriano Huerta, and all of the diplomats, lieutenants, soldiers, Indians, Spaniards, Americans, and peasants that had ever been affected by their actions and policies. One Houston paper reprinted one of her passages: "For a whole morning I sat out on a cactus covered desert of the Sinaloa listening to the story of what one man, animated by a supreme love of justice has done and suffered for his people," and then the paper quipped: "If it really was a cactus COVERED desert, and you sat on it, that man had not suffered any more than you were suffering."[24]

In one of her last missives from Mexico, Polly Pry summarized that it was Colorado that played a big part in defeating General Huerta and getting him expelled from the country. "It was Senator A. P. Ardourel of Boulder," she wrote, "who went to Washington and interested Senators Shafroth and Thomas and Congressman Keating in his cause. They got for him a golden opportunity. . . . All the world knows that the United States government refused to recognize Huerta, but only a handful know why, or why [ambassador to Mexico] Henry Lane Wilson was recalled and released from the service."[25] This was not true, as it was thoroughly reported that Wilson had supplied Huerta with arms and intelligence in an effort to install him as president. But as Polly Pry knew only too well, it never hurt to flatter a government official in her home state. And the journalist knew she was about to embark on yet another venture.

CHAPTER 13

Lakeshore, Englewood, and Poppies

"Strange that Polly Pry hasn't taken a hand in the big war," remarked a Colorado newspaper in the fall of 1914. While much of Europe and Russia were embroiled in bloody conflict, Nell Campbell was passing the time writing reviews of plays, hosting meetings for the Denver Women's Press Club, and tending to her ailing mother. Her beloved surviving brother, Roy, married for a second time in 1915 and with his wife had two little children whom Campbell doted upon. Soon, though, Campbell was trying to reestablish herself as a business owner in Denver and in the process was returning to her first love: the theater. As she did with all of her previous endeavors, Polly Pry created the opportunity for herself.

Her new business prospect came in the form of a grand auditorium that needed fresh talent to draw patrons to the Lakeside Amusement Park, located in a suburb of Denver. In 1908, Denver beer baron Adolph Zang had spearheaded a group of local businessmen who founded Lakeside as an elite summer playground wrapped around a thirty-seven-acre lake. Zang's efforts were aided by Denver mayor Robert Speer, whose "City Beautiful" movement had been transforming the hub from an "ordinary, dusty, drab Western town" into a tree-shaded, park-filled city that Speer dubbed "Paris on the Platte." To escape Denver's liquor laws, Zang incorporated Lakeside as a separate Jefferson County town with its own rules and police force. Beer flowed, of course, but Lakeside strove to maintain a wholesome reputation. In spite of Zang's restraint in marketing alcoholic beverages and Denver's rejection of dry laws in general, both the park and the city were subject to Colorado's statewide alcohol prohibition that began January 1, 1916—three years before prohibition was legislated nationally.[1]

Lakeside's inability to serve alcohol was not the only reason the park found it harder to attract patrons. When Zang originally commissioned the destination in 1908, he had hoped some of Denver's wealthier homeowners might build estates on the 103 acres of Jefferson not occupied by the amusement park, thereby helping to secure the park's elite reputation. Instead, these elite Denverites gravitated toward the Denver Country Club and Denver Polo Club neighborhoods rather than Lakeside, owing in part to the latter's border with the "tuberculosis neighborhood" of Berkeley. Also, Lakeside faced increased competition from Elitch Gardens amusement park in the West Highland neighborhood of Denver and other destinations that were becoming more accessible by the automobile. Lakeside's owners, a consortium that had purchased the park from Zang in 1913, decided to give the park a makeover to keep it competitive and in early 1916 added a large bathing beach and amenities such as sliding glass windows and new restaurants adjacent to its theater. And they decided to give the reins of this theater over to Leonel Ross Campbell, who promised to bring "a first-class company" to the dramatic portion of the park, and help make it "the only resort of prominence" that summer.[2]

On April 29, 1916, Campbell embarked on a train to the East from Denver. "I shall get the best musical comedy company there is to be had in New York," she said to a reporter. "Only first-class companies need apply at Lakeside this year."[3] The *Rocky Mountain News* noted that in the East, women producers and managers were rapidly entering the field of entertainment, intimating that it was time for Colorado to do the same. With Polly Pry's "enthusiasm and keen sense for what the public wants," there was every reason to expect that her undertaking should be successful.[4]

"In choosing her company," wrote the *Mountain News*, "Leonel Ross O'Bryan has left nothing undone that should have been done. She went after voices, and she found them. She went after dashing, melodious operas, and they are listed in her repertory. She went after stunning costumes, and trunks of them will fill the Casino wardrobe room; she went after artists of proved ability, and they head her cast."[5] She also went after investment capital, though it seems she may have had to work a little harder at securing it than she had anticipated. Denver's robust Tourist and Publicity Bureau turned down her request for seed money, noting that while it agreed her idea for a first-class comic opera company at Lakeside would be desirable, it could not advance money for what amounted to "personal enterprises." It wished her luck and hoped that she found "public spirited citizens" to invest in her endeavor.[6]

It is not clear whether Campbell found investors or not. Her file at the Denver Public Library contains many typed and handwritten receipts and letters to and from vendors and her business manager, Earl Grandy. It appears that Campbell undertook at her own expense some refurbishment of the theater, including new cloth seats and curtains, in addition to renting some rooms near Lakeside for her and any of her visiting family. She clearly wished to deliver only the highest quality entertainment to Coloradoans and in an effort to do so spent $1,000 (equal to approximately $15,000 in 2017) of her own money to hire Tommy Mohr—an agent in New York—to move west and assist her as assistant general manager:

> *I am counting on you both [Mohr and Grandy] to get both beauty and talent of a high order—and a list of stars—three at least, names and personality will make the show, and nothing else will. Naturally we are very anxious about the first bill—a new play, a clever and pretty star, pretty costumes, corking scenes and good dancing and music—with all this, the world will be ours![7]*

Campbell hired the New York Musical Comedy Company, directed by Ira Hards—one of the most prominent stage directors of the American theater at the time. Hards went on to direct Bela Lugosi in the film adaptation of *Dracula*, among scores of other productions. Hards's *M'lle Modiste*, an opera comedy in two acts, starred popular soprano Dorothy Maynard, as did his *Firefly* and *The Spring Maid*. Campbell published a new playbill each week during the summer of 1916, selling advertising space and promoting the acts she brought to the Casino Theater. "Champagne, Electricity, Romance, a dash of Victor Herbert—mix, serve—and you have LAKESIDE, THE SPARKLING CITY. Everyone admires enterprise—and particularly so when it embodies BIGNESS AND BEAUTY. We appreciate Lakeside, not only for what it is today, but for the splendid work it has done to advertise Denver as the playground of the West."[8] The champagne reference may have been tongue-in-cheek.

Campbell may have been a victim of her own success. Hards's company was so popular at Lakeside that would-be theatergoers peppered the group with complaints that they would pay to see the company perform were it not for the fact that travel to and from Lakeside was too long and uncomfortable for those who did not own automobiles. Campbell tried to book the Broadway Theater in the city's center, adjacent to the Brown Palace Hotel, her one-time residence. Her idea was to use the summer garden next to the playhouse, but alas, that was booked until the end of the season, as was every other possible venue. It is not clear whether Polly Pry or Hards cut a deal with the Tabor Grand Opera House on Sixteenth and Curtis Streets in the city center, but both took credit for this.

Campbell's comic operas received warm, if not stellar reviews—most descriptions of the plays used words and phrases like "satisfying," "scenically effective," or "prettily costumed." Dorothy Maynard was "pleasing" and "good to look upon." Unfortunately, Polly Pry's production did not last the entire summer season. On July 31, 1916, the *Post* offered some hint of its demise: "The Metropolitan Comedy company, which has sung its way into the hearts of many people, has gone onto the rocks." Despite the fact that it had been "steadily increasing business" and was starting to show some profit, the principal actors of the company and its director decided to head back East and get "back to Broadway." In all probability, the endeavor simply ran out of money. In addition to correspondence with business manager Grandy, whom Campbell often bypassed to give free tickets to people and press outlets she wished to impress, Polly Pry's file is littered with "pay in advance" notices and unhappy printers who were trying to collect payment. In what could be construed as a show of good faith and character, Campbell arranged a benefit concert in August to raise money for the show choir men and women who had been stranded in Denver when the stars of the Metropolitan left for New York. But her days as general manager of the Lakeshore Casino Theater were over.

Never one to take much time to lick her wounds, Campbell threw herself into work for the Denver Women's Press Club, organizing charity benefits and recruiting the next generation of female reporters to its ranks. At one of these events in January 1917, the reporter took special note of a speaker who took the podium after Campbell's all-female press correspondents panel. This gentleman put out a request for help with spearheading the American Red Cross's endeavors with its new Western Region office.

Campbell was fifty-seven years old when her mother, Mary Elizabeth Campbell, passed away at the age of eighty. Her obituary in the *Post* made it clear where Nell got some of her attributes. It noted that when Mrs. Campbell moved to Denver in the late 1800s for the health of her sons, she set about raising money for building its Highland neighborhood Presbyterian church, not wishing to continue attending services in a tent. "Possessed of a keen mind and broad sympathies," continued the *Post*, "Mrs. Campbell took an active interest in politics, and all those movements which aimed at the upbuilding of the community at the extension of human happiness."[9]

On January 28, 1918, Campbell was riding with Frances "Pinky" Wayne, her sister-in-law Annette Campbell, and two other newspaper friends when their automobile was struck by a streetcar that failed to slow down in order to let them pass. All suffered bumps and bruises; Nell wound up in the hospital with a broken collarbone. While convalescing at home, the reporter continued to write press releases, raise money on behalf of the American Red Cross, and dabble in land speculation in Colorado and Utah. A friend of Frederick Bonfils, one Volney Hoggatt, a promoter, gave Campbell stock in future "colonies" he tried to establish in Utah and Colorado on fertile land of murky ownership. In return, Campbell traveled to these future farm utopias, where Hoggatt intended to grow crops in addition to extracting the mineral wealth underneath. Her job was to write glowing articles about the rich soil and splendid air quality for the *Denver Post* and Hoggatt's paper, *The Great Divide*, in order to entice settlers.

Thankfully for Campbell, a better opportunity arose for her when she returned from the various unrealized counties of Colorado and Utah at the end of the summer of 1918. Ivy Lee, chief of the bureau of publicity of the Red Cross War Council appointed Campbell to serve with the publicity bureau of that organization in France. "When Mrs. O'Bryan leaves

Denver next Wednesday," wrote the *Post* on September 13, "it will lose for a time one of its most brilliant and resourceful women, and the Red Cross will gain a writer of the first order."[10] In short order, Campbell obtained a passport and on October 11, 1918, boarded a ship in New York bound for France.[11]

Objective sources relating Campbell's day-to-day activities during the last few months of World War I in Europe are largely unavailable, owing to the lack of recordkeeping in the Balkans at that time and the general confusion of war. Albania in particular was thrust into turmoil—the secret 1915 Treaty of London signed by Triple Entente powers carved up large portions of the country in exchange for fighting against the Austro-Hungarian Empire. But because Campbell's travels there can be corroborated with ship and Red Cross records, the interviews she gave her hometown newspapers upon her return can be relied upon for their accuracy—if colored by Campbell's Americentric point of view, which she may have enjoyed from the safety of an office:

Where have I been? In the Balkans, which doesn't mean much, until you have been there, but after, when you have followed the crooked trails on sea and land that lead from one of those strange little countries to another, going by sub-chasers and torpedo boats, camions and buffalo carts, troop ships and dirty Greek merchant-men, freight cars, mule-back, Deauville, horseback and automobile . . . you remember Dante and begin to understand where he got his inside information on Hell, and the Balkans suddenly become something more to you than just so many small red and yellow dabs on the map.

Everywhere conditions are about the same. Greece, Macedonia, Bulgaria, Rumania, Serbia, Dalmatia and the Montenegro. Twenty-five percent of the people living a fairly normal existence, 50 per cent trembling on the brink, struggling desperately to keep themselves independent, short of everything, food clothing, medicine, their money constantly depreciating and prices soaring, and the final 25 per cent underfed, naked wretches, sunk in an appalling poverty from which nothing but God and peace and public work can rescue them.[12]

Shortly thereafter, Campbell made a serious plea to her countrymen and countrywomen. "The war is not over for Europe. I cannot speak today of happiness or of happy things in Europe, because where I have been there are no happy faces. . . . Everything is starvation and suffering in a degree we here cannot imagine. It creates a real sorrow to see food wasted here today, for it would feed so many over there."[13]

Campbell was particularly concerned about the plight of children in the Balkans after the Great War. She had seen many left without family when German troops shelled their villages, killing their parents, or were otherwise abandoned in makeshift orphanages or even in foxholes, with little or nothing to eat. While in Europe, Campbell met Anna E. Guérin, a representative of the French YMCA Secretariat who was strongly influenced by a Canadian soldier's poem about poppies growing around the scores of burials of fallen soldiers in the Flanders battlefields. Ms. Guérin, along with Georgia native Moina Michael, considered that artificial poppies could be made and sold as a way of raising money for the benefit of the French people, especially the orphaned children, who were suffering as a result of the war. They turned to Campbell for help with making and selling artificial poppies in the Western United States to benefit the American and French Children's League.

Polly Pry was only too happy to oblige the league and set about traveling throughout Arizona, Utah, Colorado, Kansas, Wyoming, Nevada, New Mexico, Oklahoma, and Texas to promote Poppy Day, a new holiday to be held on May 29, 1921. (Other groups and states had held Poppy Day sales on an ad-hoc basis since 1915, but this was the first coordinated, nationwide effort.) One week before this day, the Western region of the American and French Children's League announced that due to Campbell's efforts, demand of poppies outstripped the supply, and volunteers would have to work overtime in order to provide enough cloth flowers to those who had ordered them.[14] The nine states comprising Campbell's southwestern region of the American and French Children's League raised an average of $30,000 each, grossing some $270,000—nearly $3 million in 2017 dollars—for the devastated regions in France and some of the surrounding areas.[15]

Campbell's travels and tireless fundraising took a toll on her body. She had suffered a debilitating case of pneumonia when she started planning Poppy Day a few months before the May 29 event, and her doctor had warned that continuing to work at her usual pace could mean an early death. The dynamo took a few months to recuperate but simply could not stop working. She held benefits for World War I servicemen who found themselves unemployed when they returned to Denver, and she traveled through Utah and Wyoming giving speeches for Republican causes. Campbell even toyed with the idea of moving to Washington, DC, with Ellis Meredith, who had moved there to work for the Democratic National Committee (DNC). Her letters reflect the pair's ongoing discussions of political machinations in the nation's capital: "Mrs. W. strikes me as being fifty-seven varieties of an idiot," Campbell wrote of former first lady Edith Wilson's DNC work, "when it lay in her power to do so splendid interesting and amusing a thing, to let it slip seems sheer folly; however, the world's made up of fools and us, and we might as well admit it."[16]

Campbell decided to stay in Denver, where the weather was more to her liking and where she could be closer to her beloved niece and nephew. Besides, a new industry had landed in Denver, and Campbell was determined to be a part of it. While she was in Europe for her work on behalf of the Red Cross, a consortium of film producers and businessmen had come to Denver with $50,000 in capital. They bought land in nearby Englewood and aggressively advertised for investors week after week in the Denver papers: "Now is the time and Denver is unquestionably the place for such an enterprise. Climate and atmospheric conditions are ideal. . . . Stock in the company is now $10 per share. A few months from now holders of these shares will probably refuse to sell for ten times the price. . . . This company will do for Denver what other motion picture companies have done for Los Angeles."[17] In the early 1920s, other film companies began keeping offices in Denver, too, because of the region's long, cloudless days that made for ideal shooting conditions, and because its citizens were willing to invest hundreds of thousands of their own dollars in return for getting in on the ground floor of a booming industry that created jobs for their neighbors.[18]

Campbell purchased a correspondence course in "motion picture scenario writing" from one of the local film exchange companies but quickly decided she could do more than be just a supplier of scripts to someone else's company. She wrote Ellis Meredith about her plans, most certainly to include her in a possible venture but also to let her know a bit of money would not be turned away:

> *We, Mary [Bradford, a school superintendent] and myself, are maybe going to be associated together with the Super Film Company, owing [to] the Englewood Studio and making pictures solely for churches and schools, educational and religious things. If we are, I shall let you know all about it at once, because I see a chance in case this deal goes over of your doing some fine Bible pictures, nobody knows their little book better than you do, and this will be a place where that knowledge can be applied, wherefore, I shall send you the S. O. S. as soon as I can. I am to have (if I accept it) complete charge of the publicity campaign for the world. How would you like to go in on that with me, if it looks big?*[19]

It seems the enterprise did not come to fruition, though this may have had less to do with Campbell's creative or business acumen than it did with the glut of educational films already being produced at Englewood, and the onerous censorship process to which these reels were subjected by various progressive groups before they were able to come to market.

Nell Campbell, in her sixty-fourth year of life in 1923, began to finally, truly slow down. She turned her attention to writing her memoirs and a comprehensive history of the *Denver Post*, though neither of these have ever been found.

Over the next decade, Campbell saw developments in her beloved Denver that she could hardly have imagined when she first arrived in 1898. In March of 1922, the first commercial radio station began transmitting from Denver; by the end of the decade, nearly 60 percent of American homes had a radio to listen in on current events right as they were happening. By 1925, Ku Klux Klan members controlled the Colorado state house and senate, as well as scores of judgeships and city councils. Opened to rail traffic in 1928, the Moffat Tunnel shortened the trip between Denver and Salt Lake City by eight hours, placing Denver on a transcontinental route for the first time. The first Denver municipal airport opened on October 17, 1929.

In 1930, Campbell's brother Roy separated from his wife and moved to Los Angeles, lured by real estate speculation and an even warmer climate. The fearless reporter remained close with her sister-in-law Annette and the niece and nephew she adored so much. She doted on them with gifts, even when money was tight and she could no longer pay for the upkeep on her Osceola Street home and had to move into some rooms on Seventeenth Street. "But she'd always had money," Annette recalled decades later, "and she could never accept the fact that it might run out. When she'd get a check for $10 or $20, she'd call me and say, 'Get yourself fixed up pretty, and come downtown. We're going to have a party.'" A "party," Annette said, meant lunch at the old Daniels and Fisher department store tearoom on Sixteenth Street or Bauer's on Curtis Street. "She loved nice places, and it never mattered if there weren't any groceries the next day."[20] Campbell still went to Denver Women's Press Club meetings, even when hypertension exhausted her.

In 1935, Ishbel Ross, a Scottish-born reporter whose career spanned more than six decades, took it upon herself to start compiling a volume of American women she felt made the most important journalistic contributions in history up until that point. Campbell was one of them. "A gentle old lady occasionally wanders into the Denver Public Library nowadays," Ross wrote, "and digs about among the books in the Western History Collection. Her eyes have a mournful beauty, for they have seen uncanny things. It is difficult for a younger generation to believe that this is the Polly Pry of legend—wild, beautiful, fearless."[21]

On July 15, 1938, Nell Campbell suffered a heart attack at her home and subsequently entered St. Joseph hospital. In a story about her death the next day, the *Denver Post* said that "a moment before passing, with characteristic energy, she raised herself from the bed and said to the attending nurse, 'I must be up and—.'"

Per reporter and author Gene Fowler, her one-time contemporary and occasional rival, Leonel Ross Campbell Anthony O'Bryan was "a great and tender character with courage unbounded." Even during her last moments, according to friend and colleague Pinky Wayne, Campbell was still conscious that there were more "stories to be scooped," and Pinky supposed that even in death she "ached to be first on the scene."[22]

In 2011, Campbell was posthumously inducted into the Denver Press Club Hall of Fame—an award she might or might not have coveted, depending on how she felt about whomever was president of the organization at the time. What would matter to her the most is that she had paved the way for women journalists who came after her to sit proudly in their newsrooms or at the helm of their own business, knowing that they had just as much to contribute to the field as any male colleague. No one wrote the West quite like Polly Pry.

NOTES

Introduction

1 "Two Shots at Polly Pry . . .", *Colorado Springs Gazette*, January 11, 1904, 1; "Two Shots Fired at Polly Pry by Unknown Assassin," *Denver Post*, January 11, 1904, 1; Barbara Belford, *Brilliant Bylines: A Biographical Anthology of Notable Newspaperwomen in America* (New York: Columbia University Press, 1986), 59–60.

2 Ibid.

3 *Denver Post*, April 21, 1900, 3.

4 Sue Hubbell, "Polly Pry Did Not Just Report the News; She *Made* It," *Smithsonian Magazine*, January 1991, 48.

5 Winifred Black occasionally freelanced for the *Denver Post* before Campbell's arrival, but she was not on staff.

6 Campbell, *Polly Pry*, July 29, 1905, 5, Series 1: Professional 1902–1928 Box 1–2, Leonel Ross Anthony O'Bryan (Polly Pry) Papers, WH 280, Western History Collection, The Denver Public Library.

7 Campbell, *Polly Pry*, October 3, 1903, 18, Series 1: Professional 1902–1928 Box 1–2, Leonel Ross Anthony O'Bryan (Polly Pry) Papers, WH 280, Western History Collection, The Denver Public Library.

8 Belford, *Brilliant Bylines*, 56–57; Polly Pry, "John Chinaman in New York," *Denver Post*, January 7, 1900, 13.

9 Campbell, *Polly Pry*, October 24, 1903, 4, Series 1: Professional 1902–1928 Box 1–2, Leonel Ross Anthony O'Bryan (Polly Pry) Papers, WH 280, Western History Collection, The Denver Public Library.

10 Campbell, *Polly Pry*, October 3, 1903, 18, Series 1: Professional 1902–1928 Box 1–2, Leonel Ross Anthony O'Bryan (Polly Pry) Papers, WH 280, Western History Collection, The Denver Public Library.

Chapter 1: Old Mexico, New York

1 Sue Hubbell, "Polly Pry Did Not Just Report the News; She Made It," *Smithsonian*, January 1991, 48.

2 *Leavenworth Times*, May 17, 1877, 2.

3 *Leavenworth Times*, 1873–1883.

4 E.g., *Leavenworth Times*, September 13, 1874, 2; August 14, 1877, 4. While these observations of Anthony Jr.'s behavior were reliable, they were a bit biased, part of a larger agenda of the *Times* and particularly its owner. D. R. and George Tobey had gotten along fairly well as family until the mid-1870s, when the former began accusing his cousin of graft, bribery, and cronyism. Their relationship never repaired and D. R.'s outspoken criticism of George Tobey in the *Times* kept him from a second term in office.

5 "A Flavor of Romance . . .," *Topeka Daily Capital*, reprinting the *St. Louis Globe Democrat*, August 5, 1883, 3.

6 Ibid.

7 Edwin Brownson Everitt, *Tour of the St. Elmo's: From the Nutmeg State to the Golden Gate* (Meriden, CT: Meriden Book Bindery, 1883).

8 Ibid.

9 Ibid. Campbell continued to write about the fleas here, convinced that her hotel was the "breeding place for all the world's fleas."

10 Barbara Belford, *Brilliant Bylines: A Biographical Anthology of Notable Newspaperwomen in America* (New York: Columbia University Press, 1986), 56.

11 Campbell as Polly Pry, "Glimpses of Old Mexico," *Denver Post*, December 31, 1899, Polly Pry Papers.

12 Ibid.

13 E.g., see Mary Lou Pence, *The Women Who Made the West/Polly Pry* (Garden City, NY: Doubleday, 1980).

14 E.g., "A Typical Town . . . Effect of a Norther," *Chicago Daily Tribune*, December 22, 1883, 11.

15 Campbell as Polly Pry, "Glimpses of Old Mexico in the Days Before the Railroads," *Denver Post*, December 31, 1899. Polly Pry Papers, Denver Public Library, Western History Collection.

16 Denver Public Library, Western History Collection, WH280, Leonel Ross Anthony O'Bryan (Polly Pry) Papers, Box 2, FF14; *Brown County World*, June 24, 1898, 12.

17 "Polly Pry on the Colorado World's Fair Commission," *Colorado Transcript*, May 14, 1903, 2.

Chapter 2: Colorado, A Cave of Whispers

1 Bill Hosokawa, *Thunder in the Rockies: The Incredible Denver Post* (New York: William Morrow, 1976).

2 Mort Stern, *Looking for a People's Champion: A Search for the Real Harry Tammen* (Denver, CO, 1989), 43.

3 *Profitable Advertising*, Vol. 1, No. 1 (Boston, MA), June 1891, 101.

4 Bill Hosokawa, *Thunder in the Rockies: The Incredible Denver Post* (New York: William Morrow, 1976), 16–18.

5 Stern, *Looking for a People's Champion*, 42–44.

6 Ibid., 46.

7 *(Denver) Rocky Mountain News*, March 10, 1895, 6.

8 Robert L. Perkin, *The First Hundred Years: An Informal History of Denver and the Rocky Mountain News* (Garden City, NY: Doubleday, 1959), 407–408.

9 As described by Ernest Hamlin Abbott in the *Outlook*, a weekly magazine published in New York City that emphasized social and political issues (October 1902).

10 Roland L. DeLorme, "Turn-of-the-Century Denver: An Invitation to Reform," *The Colorado Magazine*, 1968, 1–5.

11 Ibid., 4.

12 https://history.denverlibrary.org/polly-pry-1857-1938 (retrieved August 24, 2017); Lemuel F. Parton, "Brash Young Editors Boldly Challenged Denver," *Omaha World-Herald*, February 3, 1933, 19.

13 "Polly Pry Visits Mr. Thomas and Talks of His Senatorial Aspirations," *Denver Post*, August 13, 1898, 5.

14 "Polly Pry Visits Mayor McMurray And Has A Five Minutes Chat," *Denver Post*, August 14, 1898, 5.

15 "Polly Pry Has a Red-Hot Encounter With Dean Hart," *Denver Post*, September 15, 1898, 7.

16 Ibid.

17 See Peter Pagnamenta, *Prairie Fever: British Aristocrats in the American West, 1830–1890* (New York: W. W. Norton), 2012.

18 "Breezy Polly Pry Tells A Juicy Story of the Mormon Elders," *Denver Post*, September 7, 1899, 5.

19 *Polly Pry*, October 22, 1899, 7.

20 "Polly Pry Takes a Dainty Squint at the Woman in Politics," *Denver Post*, April 9, 1899, 11.

21 Column "Good and Bad Things Said about the Post," *Denver Post*, October 6, 1899, 13.

Chapter 3: A Cannibal and Ol' Plug Hat

1 The most comprehensive account of Packer's life and trials is Harold Schechter's *Man-Eater: The Life and Legend of An American Cannibal* (New York: Little A, 2015). See also Matt Masich, "The Mystery of Alfred Packer," *Colorado Life Magazine*, http://www.coloradolifemagazine.com/The-Mystery-of-Alfred-Packer/index.php?cparticle=4&siarticle=3 (retrieved July 26, 2017).

2 An oft-repeated explanation for Packer's spelling of his first name "Alfred" as "Alferd" is that it was misspelled in a tattoo he received, and he thought it quaint and used "Alferd" from then on. The author uses his birth name "Alfred" for consistency's sake.

3 Masich, "The Mystery of Alfred Packer."

4 The "red-headed man" refers to prospector Shannon Wilson Bell; "German butcher Mills" refers to prospector Frank Mills.

5 "Packer, the Man Eater, Arrives in Denver," *Denver Rocky Mountain News*, March 17, 1883, 8.

6 Judge [Melville B.] Gerry's Death Sentence of [Alfred] Packer, Hinsdale District Court, Case #1883DC379, https://www.colorado.gov/pacific/sites/default/files/A%20Packer%20Judge%20Gerry%20Death%20Sentence%20to%20Packer_0.pdf (retrieved July 27, 2017).

7 Polly Pry, "Some of the Strange and Pathetic Sights She Saw—Human Tragedies Which Struck A Chill to the Heart . . .," *Denver Post*, May 21, 1899, 9.

8 Ibid.

9 Ibid.

10 "Packer's Strange Case," *Denver Post*, May 22, 1899, 4.

11 "The Packer Case Told From Another Point of View," *Denver Post*, May 28, 1899, 4; "County Treasurer Deeble Once Again on the Packer Case," *Denver Post*, June 3, 1899, 3.

12 *Denver Post*, July 23, 1899, 15.

13 "Pardon or Parole?" *Denver Post*, July 23, 1899, 15.

14 "Anderson Case Goes to the Jury," *Denver Post*, July 27, 1901, 5.

15 "Polly Pry Tells of the Insane Man . . ." Polly Pry, *Denver Post*, January 3, 1900.

16 "Packer Must Stay in Prison," *Denver Rocky Mountain News*, December 9, 1899, 1.

17 Hosokawa, *Thunder in the Rockies*, 97.

18 Ibid.

19 Ibid.; "Polly Pry's Statement," *Denver Post*, January 13, 1900, 1.

20 Ibid.

21 Hosokawa, *Thunder in the Rockies*, 97–98; "Statement of H. H. Tammen," *Denver Rocky Mountain News*, January 14, 1900, 1. Oddly, this exact verbiage does not appear in the *Post*, although many, many other accounts do and would continue to do until the spring of 1900. The reason for this may be that although the *Post* and the *Mountain News* were rivals in a circulation battle, the *Mountain News*, like many other Colorado newspapers, was so disturbed by the public reaction to the shooting that it was moved to publish generous and sympathetic editorials about it. When the *Mountain News* called the *Post* for comment, the *Post* may have supplied some additional quotes such as the one in which Tammen referred to Pry's heroism. He would continue to do so all the way up to Anderson's trial in April 1900.

22 E.g., *The* (Chicago) *Inter Ocean*, April 29, 1900, 3.

23 *Denver Post*, July 24, 1901, 3.

24 Gene Fowler, *Timber Line* (Sausalito, CA: Comstock Book Distributors, 1974).

25 Hosokawa, *Thunder in the Rockies*, 104–106; *Denver Post* July 26, 1901, 1.

26 Chronic kidney disease.

27 Governor Charles S. Thomas's Conditional Parole, Colorado State Archives, History Collections (Alferd Packer), Colorado.gov.

28 Polly Pry, "Justice for Alfred Packer . . .," *Denver Post*, January 8, 1901, 1.

Chapter 4: Around the World with Polly Pry

1 "Polly Pry's Triumph," *St. Louis Post-Dispatch*, January 11, 1901, 6.

2 Polly Pry, "Chicago From Two Points of View," *Denver Post*, January 28, 1900, 20.

3 Polly Pry, "Is the American Man So Inferior to the American Woman," March 4, 1900, 20; Polly Pry, "Jack Martin—A Dream," *Denver Post*, April 4, 1901, 15; "Convention Notes," *Deseret Evening News*, January 14, 1901, 4.

4 The 1900 Exposition Universelle was the fifth one to take place in Paris. It opened April 14 and closed November 12, 1900, celebrating the achievements of the century prior and accelerating development into the next.

5 "Polly Pry's European Letters," *Denver Post*, May 27, 1900, 4.

6 "Polly Pry Tells of Fashions for Spring," *Denver Post*, March 17, 1901, 10.

7 Ibid.

8 Polly Pry, "One Night in Paris" and "Polly Pry Sees the Dark Side of Paris Life," *Denver Post*, September 9 and 10, 1900, 1. Oversize Scrapbooks 1898–1917, Leonel Ross Anthony O'Bryan (Polly Pry) Papers, WH 280, Western History Collection, The Denver Public Library.

9 "Polly Pry's European Letters," *Denver Post*, May 27, 1900, 4.

10 *Lyons Recorder*, June 28, 1900, 2.

11 See Morrell Heald, *Transatlantic Vistas: American Journalists in Europe, 1900–1940* (Kent, OH: Kent State University Press, 1988).

12 Petra S. McGillen, *The Conversation*, https://theconversation.com/profiles/petra-s -mcgillen-353447 (accessed August 14, 2017).

13 Ibid.

14 Ibid.

15 Ibid.

16 Polly Pry, "Polly Pry's Visit to Antwerp to See Its Art Treasures," October 21, 1900, n.p., Oversize Scrapbooks 1898–1917, Leonel Ross Anthony O'Bryan (Polly Pry) Papers, WH 280, Western History Collection, The Denver Public Library.

17 Polly Pry, "Polly Pry Takes in the Sights of the German Capital," *Denver Post*, October 7, 1900, n.p., Oversize Scrapbooks 1898–1917, Leonel Ross Anthony O'Bryan (Polly Pry) Papers, WH 280, Western History Collection, The Denver Public Library.

18 Polly Pry, "What Polly Pry Saw in Old Vienna," December 16, 1900, n.p., Oversize Scrapbooks 1898–1917, Leonel Ross Anthony O'Bryan (Polly Pry) Papers, WH 280, Western History Collection, The Denver Public Library.

19 Ibid.

20 Some of her European pieces, notably those from Rome, ran in the *Post* in both December of 1900 and January and February of 1901. Oversize Scrapbooks 1898–1917, Leonel Ross Anthony O'Bryan (Polly Pry) Papers, WH 280, Western History Collection, The Denver Public Library.

Chapter 5: Tom Horn and Vincent St. John

1 Polly Pry, "The Murderer of Harold Fridborn and Assailant of Sister . . .," *Denver Post*, January 2, 1902, 1.

2 *Denver Post*, January 3, 1902, 1.

3 *Denver Post*, February 23, 1902, 40–41.

4 See, e.g., Chip Carlson, "Misunderstood Misfit," *Wild West Magazine*, June 12, 2006, http://www.historynet.com/tom-horn-misunderstood-misfit.htm (retrieved August 17, 2017).

5 Ibid.; Chip Carlson, http://www.wyohistory.org/encyclopedia/tom-horn-wyoming -enigma (retrieved August 17, 2017).

6 Ibid.

7 Ibid.

8 John W. Davis, *The Trial of Tom Horn* (Norman: University of Oklahoma Press, 2016), 65–67.

9 Polly Pry, *Denver Post*, March 2, 1902, 1.

10 *Denver Post*, March 2, 1902, 1; see also *The Trial of Tom Horn*, 65–66.

11 Ibid.

12 Davis, *The Trial of Tom Horn*, 65–67; Polly Pry, "Appalling Record of Wyoming's Rustler Assassinations," *Denver Post*, March 2, 1902, 1.

13 Larry D. Ball, *Tom Horn in Life and Legend* (Norman: University of Oklahoma Press, 2015), 263–264. Sheep were a problem if they were brought into land set aside for

cattle because sheep crop grass much more closely to the soil surface. After sheep feed from a pasture, it is fairly useless for bovines until after more rain falls—which could be a long time in arid Wyoming.

14 Davis, *The Trial of Tom Horn*, 325.

15 Polly Pry, "When Is Five Cents Worth $12,000?," *Denver Post*, October 20, 1902, 1.

16 Letter from C. De Bennett to Leonel Campbell, October 22, 1902. Polly Pry Papers, Western History Collection, Denver Public Library.

17 Davis, *The Trial of Tom Horn*, 238–239.

18 Ibid., 239.

19 Cameron Yancy provides a good summary of the complicated events of this time period in Telluride: "'Kill the Anarchists': Telluride's Red Scare—How One Rogue Newspaper Editor Ran a Smear Campaign against the Local Miner's Union in the Early 20th Century," *The Watch* column, Telluridenews.com: http://www .telluridenews.com/the_watch/article_f86ca47e-5252-11e5-8886-2bd0ddba3b3a .html (accessed April 16, 2018).

20 Ibid.

21 Juan Conatz, "'I Never Met a Man I Admired More': Vincent St. John (1876–1929)," Lesser Known Wobblies series, libcom.org: https://libcom.org/ library/"i-never-met-man-i-admired-more"-vincent-st-john-1876–1929.

22 Polly Pry, *Denver Post*, November 27, 1902, 1.

23 Ibid.

24 It is not clear to which newspaper "The *News*" refers. "Polly Pry's Interview with President St. John," *Telluride Daily Journal*, November 28, 1902, 1.

25 Repeated in the *Denver Post*, November 28, 1902, 1.

26 "Polly Pry Prevaricates," *San Miguel Examiner*, November 29, 1901, 1.

27 "Note by Editor," *Denver Post*, November 28, 1902, 1.

28 "Polly Pry Interviews O. B. Kemp on the Collins Murder . . .," *Denver Post*, November 30, 1902, 1.

29 Ibid.

30 "So the People May Know," *Denver Post*, February 21, 1903, 1.

Chapter 6: Parting Ways with the Post

1 Frank Lundy Webster, "Post Collects Startling Evidence against Fort Lewis School Officials," *Denver Post*, April 23, 1903, 1.

2 Ibid.

3 Polly Pry, "Polly Pry Lays Bare the Evils of the Fort Lewis Indian School . . .," *Denver Post*, March 21, 1903, 16.

4 Frank Webster, "Denver Post Demands Supt. Breen's Immediate Removal," *Denver Post*, April 23, 1903, 1.

5 "Supt. Breen Dismissed and Charges of Post Proven," *Denver Post*, July 27, 1903, 4.

6 Barbara Belford, *Brilliant Bylines: A Biographical Anthology of Notable Newspaperwomen in America* (New York: Columbia University Press), 1986, 57.

7 http://www.cripplecreekrailroads.com/01main/history/articles/1904–03–10 -independent-p539_great_cc_strike.php (accessed September 1, 2017).

8 Polly Pry, *Polly Pry*, November 28, 1903, 8.

9 *Denver Post*, April 12, 1903, 9.

10 Polly Pry, *Denver Post*, "Polly Pry Explains the World's Fair Situation," February 11, 1903, 11.

11 "What It Costs to Name the Colorado," *Chicago Inter Ocean*, April 26, 1903, 57.

12 To be a political majority on a World's Fair commission carried a certain amount of inherent prestige, but also, it allowed those in the majority to offer competitive bidding for exhibit projects among past and future campaign donors.

13 "What It Costs to Name the 'Colorado,'" *Chicago Inter Ocean*, April 26, 1903, 57.

14 Syndicated article, "Polly Pry on the World's Fair Commission." E.g., (Golden) *Colorado Transcript*, May 14, 1903, 2.

Chapter 7: Tell the Truth and Shame the Devil

1 E.g., *The Topeka Daily Capital*, July 7, 1893, 2; The *Daily Chronicle* (DeKalb, Illinois), January 30, 1896, 3.

2 E.g., "Woman Founds Journal," *Brooklyn Eagle*, September 5, 1903.

3 Ibid.

4 Frederick White, "About Different Methods of Obtaining Success," (Sunday) *Denver Post*, August 9, 1903, 13.

5 *Salida Record*, September 18, 1903, 1.

6 *Denver Post*, September 5, 1903, 12.

7 *Polly Pry*, September 5, 1903, 10, Series 1: Professional 1902–1928 Box 1–2. Leonel Ross Anthony O'Bryan (Polly Pry) Papers, WH 280, Western History Collection, The Denver Public Library.

8 *Polly Pry*, December 5, 1903, 14; January 9, 1904, 12; January 16, 1904, 13, Series 1: Professional 1902–1928 Box 1–2. Leonel Ross Anthony O'Bryan (Polly Pry) Papers, WH 280, Western History Collection, The Denver Public Library.

9 Ibid., 1.

10 "The Polly Pry," *Aspen Daily Times*, September 6, 1903, 2.

Chapter 8: Mining Wars, Murder, and Mother Jones, Part I

1 "Two Shots Fired at Polly Pry . . .," *Denver Post*, January 11, 1904, 1.

2 Ibid.

3 Ibid.

4 Ibid.

5 Ibid.

6 Ibid.

7 "Just a Bit of Gunplay," (Denver) *Rocky Mountain News*, January 12, 1904, 11.

8 Ibid.

9 Polly Pry, *Polly Pry*, January 16, 1904, 4.

10 For more information, see Candy Moulton, "Pike's Peak or Bust: The Rush for Gold Excited a Nation," *True West* (August 2004), and https://www.mininghistoryassociation.org/CrippleCreek.htm.

11 For more, see Carl Ubbelohde, Maxine Benson, and Duane Smith, "The Era of Industrial Warfare," in *A Colorado History* (Boulder, CO: Pruett, 2001).

12 For more information about the Cripple Creek conflicts and the Colorado Labor Wars in general, see *The Colorado Labor Wars, 1903–1904*, edited by Tim Blevins, Chris Nicholl, and Calvin P. Otto (Colorado Springs: Pikes Peak Library District, 2006). The essay "Is Colorado in America?: Emma Langdon, Polly Pry and the Colorado Labor Wars" by Bridget Burke is especially helpful in framing the work of these two female journalists.

13 Polly Pry, *Polly Pry*, January 30, 1904, 3.

14 In fact, WFM member Harry Orchard described how he and an accomplice carried out the espionage in a confession in *McClure's Magazine*, August 1907, Vol. 29, No. 4, 375–379.

15 Campbell, "Polly Pry," *Polly Pry*, November 28, 1903, inside cover.

16 Burke, "Is Colorado in America?," 53.

17 Campbell, "On the Midway," *Polly Pry*, November 28, 1903, 2.

18 Ibid., 3.

19 Burke, "Is Colorado in America?," 58.

20 Ibid., *Polly Pry*, January 30, 1904, 8.

Chapter 9: Mining Wars, Murder, and Mother Jones, Part II

1 Elliot J. Gorn's book Mother Jones: The Most Dangerous Woman in America (New York: Hill and Wang, 2001), is the most recent, definitive biography of Jones.

2 Ibid.

3 Mary Harris Jones, *Autobiography of Mother Jones* (North Chelmsford, MA: Courier Corporation, 2012), 1–10, 54–55.

4 Ibid., 55.

5 This was most likely a disambiguation of Jones's usual rallying cry, which was some version of, "We would rather fight [for industrial freedom; for our children; against wrongs, etc.] than work [under these conditions, etc.]."

6 Polly Pry, *Polly Pry*, January 2, 1904, 3–4. As Gorn discusses in *Mother Jones*, these accusations are fairly ludicrous, considering Jones's advanced age even in 1889 (fifty-two) when she was allegedly a madam. Neither a "Mary Jones" nor a "Mary Harris" shows up in any Denver police records for that time. More generally, tarring a woman with the brush of promiscuity was common practice for those denigrating women activists at that time.

7 Ibid.

8 Gorn, *Mother Jones*, 111.

9 Italian Archives, 1897–1978, J. Willard Marriott Library, Special Collections, Manuscripts Division, University of Utah Library.

10 Polly Pry, *Polly Pry*, January 2, 1904, 3–5.

11 Bell was often the "comic relief of the strike," owing to his preference for elaborate military costuming and for being completely devoid of humor—one newspaper called him the "bumptious warrior of Colorado." Many papers mocked him for these affects, and *Polly Pry* was no different. Still, Campbell received many long-winded

letters from Adjutant Bell, who went to so far as to praise *Polly Pry* as the "best publication in the world today."

12 "Favor Criminal Action against Gov. Peabody," *Denver Post*, January 4, 1904, 8.

13 Polly Pry, *Polly Pry*, February 6, 1904, 3.

14 A particularly frenzied diagnosis of the danger of WFM and UMW taking over Colorado appears in the January 9, 1904, issue of *Polly Pry*.

15 A few of these exist in Campbell's files at the Denver Public Library.

16 Burke, "Is Colorado in America?," 63.

17 "Mrs. Anthony, Who Writes under Nom de Plume, Discusses Unionism Here," *Indianapolis Journal*, February 24, 1904, 6.

18 Simon Cordery, *Raising Cain and Consciousness* (Albuquerque: University of New Mexico Press, 2010).

19 Mary Harris Jones, *Autobiography of Mother Jones* (reprint), (North Chelmsford, MA: Courier Corporation, 2012), 66.

20 Gorn, *Mother Jones*, 111.

21 Bill Haywood, *Bill Haywood's Book: The Autobiography of William D. Haywood* (New York: International Publishers, 1929), 135.

Chapter 10: The Business of Polly Pry

1 "'Confessions' of Silberberg: Romance Tinged with Truth," *Minneapolis Journal*, January 2, 1904, 9.

2 "Alleged Blackmail Scheme Recalls Swindler's Career . . .," *Colorado Springs Gazette*, April 23, 1904, 1.

3 *Polly Pry*, March 1904–June 1904.

4 Letter, Leonel Ross Campbell to Simon Guggenhiem, March 3, 1904. Polly Pry Papers, Denver Public Library, Western History Collection.

5 Letter, Leonel Ross Campbell to E. B. Smith, March 3, 1904. Polly Pry Papers, Denver Public Library, Western History Collection.

6 See Carl Ubbelohde, Maxine Benson, and Duane Smith, "The Progressive Era," in *A Colorado History* (Boulder, CO: Pruett, 2001).

7 Ibid.

8 Polly Pry, *Polly Pry*, March 26, 1904, 4.

9 Ibid.

10 Ibid.

11 Polly Pry, *Polly Pry*, April 2, 1904, 36.

12 Ibid.

13 Arthur Wellington Brayley et al., *National Magazine* (Boston, MA: Chapple, January 1908), 598.

14 Polly Pry, *Polly Pry*, August 27, 1904, 6.

15 Letter from Ellis Meredith to Leonel Campbell Ross, not dated but probably 1905 given the reference to Campbell's New York venture, which she attempted in August 1905. Elsewhere in the letter, Meredith refers to Campbell's dealings with Gen. Sherman Bell. Polly Pry Papers, Denver Public Library, Western History Collection.

16 *Telluride Journal*, September 28, 1905, 3.

17 Letter from Gertrude (last name unknown) to Campbell. Undated but given its indication of Campbell trying to start a new business, was probably between the end of *Polly Pry*'s run in 1905 and 1907, when Campbell began a playwriting career in earnest.

18 Letter from Ellis Meredith to Campbell. Undated but given its indication of Campbell trying to start a new business, was probably between 1905 and 1907.

19 Ibid.

20 Letter from Gertrude (last name unknown) to Campbell. Undated but probably between 1905 and 1907.

21 "Pretty Mamie O'Bryan Appeals for a Divorce," *Albuquerque Citizen*, October 13, 1905, 7.

22 "Chill Autumn Days . . .," *Denver Post*, September 30, 1900, 13.

23 "Jury Likens Was on Witness Stand," *Denver Post*, August 16, 1901, 2.

24 *Denver Post*, August 27, 1903, 1.

25 "H. J. O'Bryan is Defendant," *Denver Post*, October 12, 1905, 5.

26 *Denver Rocky Mountain News*, October 13, 1905, 9.

27 "Charges Non-Support," *Denver Post*, October 12, 1905, 5.

28 Ibid.

29 "Court Grants Henry J. O'Bryan Privilege of Pursuing Those Pleasures Alone," *Denver Post*, November 7, 1905, 1.

30 "Polly Pry Is Sued for Payment of $1,184.25," *Denver Rocky Mountain News*, October 9, 1906.

31 "Mrs. O'Bryan Asks Divorce," *Denver Rocky Mountain News*, January 29, 1914, 6.

Chapter 11: Polly Pry and Pancho Villa, Part I

1 Eselyn Brown, "In Denver Society," *Denver Post*, November 15, 1906, 6. Brown would later become president of the Denver Women's Press Club (1913–1914).

2 Polly Pry, *Polly Pry*, March 26, 1904, 6.

3 Polly Pry, *Denver Post*, March 13, 1904, 7; Polly Pry, *Polly Pry*, April 9, 1904, 4.

4 "Polly Pry's Play," *Denver Post*, June 24, 1908, 9.

5 Polly Pry, "Black Faces of the Soldiers Most Welcome Sight on Earth," *Denver Post*, June 15, 1908, 8.

6 Ibid.

7 Frances Wayne, "Four Varieties," *Denver Post*, June 21, 1908, 48.

8 *Denver Post*, June 29, 1908, 6.

9 E.g., *Denver Post*, June 21, 1908, 48; June 24, 1908, 9; July 1, 1908, 9.

10 Leonel Ross Campbell Anthony O'Bryan, March 26, 1914, US Passport Applications, Ancestry.com.

11 For a concise yet detailed summary of the conflict, see Alan Knight, "The Mexican Revolution," *History Today*, Vol. 30, issue 5 (May 5, 1980): http://www.historytoday.com/alan-knight/mexican-revolution.

12 Ibid.

13 Nancy Brandt, "Pancho Villa: The Making of a Modern Legend," *The Americas*, Vol 2, issue 2 (October 1964), 146–162. There are many more recent and comprehensive

works about Villa (see, e.g., Friedrich Katz's *The Life and Times of Pancho Villa* [Stanford, CA: Stanford University Press, 1988]), but Brandt's work remains one of the most oft-cited in discussion of him.

14 "The Truth about Mexico," *Indianapolis Star*, April 18, 1914, 1.

15 Letter from Alberto Pico to Geo. W. Vallery, April 14, 1914. Polly Pry Papers, Denver Public Library, Western History Collection.

16 See Sean Braswell, "The American Reporter Who Rode with Pancho Villa," http://www.ozy.com/search?searchozy=Reed.

17 Brandt, "Pancho Villa," 154.

Chapter 12: Polly Pry and Pancho Villa, Part II

1 Polly Pry, "May Yet Lead Army against Nations of the World, Chief Boast[s]," *Denver Times*, April 21, 1914, 2. Polly Pry Papers, Denver Public Library, Western History Collection.

2 Polly Pry, *Denver Times*, April 19, 1914, n.p. Polly Pry Papers, Denver Public Library, Western History Collection.

3 "Reports Say Villa Leads 20,000 Soldiers to Victory," Polly Pry, *The Denver Times*, April 20, 1914, 1.

4 Correctly spelled "Sommerfeld," he was a secret service agent in Mexico and the United States between 1908 and 1919. Both his origins and his demise are still mysteries today.

5 Ibid.

6 Polly Pry, "Polly Pry Sees Men Die as Rebel Chief Jeers at Their Agony," *Denver Times*, n.d. (April 1914), n.p. Polly Pry Papers, Denver Public Library, Western History Collection.

7 Polly Pry, "May Yet Lead Army against Nations of the World, Chief Boast[s]," *Denver Times*, April 21, 1914, 1. Polly Pry Papers, Denver Public Library, Western History Collection.

8 See John Reed's "What about Mexico?" treatise: http://historymatters.gmu.edu/d/4948/.

9 Polly Pry, "May Yet Lead Army against Nations of the World, Chief Boast[s]," *Denver Times*, April 21, 1914, 1. Polly Pry Papers, Denver Public Library, Western History Collection.

10 "Ruthless Killing by Mexican Bandit," *Denver Times*, April 23, 1914, n.p. Polly Pry Papers, Denver Public Library, Western History Collection.

11 (Headline obscured), *Denver Times*, April 20, 1914, 1. Polly Pry Papers, Denver Public Library, Western History Collection.

12 "With Drink-Crazed Huerta . . .," *Denver Times*, April 30, 1914, n.p.

13 Polly Pry, "Madero a Visionary . . .," *Denver Times*, April, 1914, n.p. Polly Pry Papers, Denver Public Library, Western History Collection.

14 Polly Pry, *Denver Times*, April 1914 (scrapbook torn; article pasted next to it is dated April 15, 1914). Polly Pry Papers, Denver Public Library, Western History Collection.

15 Polly Pry, "May Yet Lead Army against Nations of the World, Chief Boast[s]," *Denver Times*, April 21, 1914, 2. Polly Pry Papers, Denver Public Library, Western History Collection.

16 Ibid.

17 Ibid., 3.

18 Polly Pry, "May Yet Lead Army against Nations of the World, Chief Boast[s]," *Denver Times*, April 21, 1914, 2. Polly Pry Papers, Denver Public Library, Western History Collection.

19 Polly Pry, "Polly Pry Gathers More Facts by Risking Her Life in Mexico," *Indianapolis Star*, July 17, 1914, 1.

20 "30,000 Japs on Mexican Coast . . .," *Denver Times* article as reprinted in the *Indianapolis Star*, July 22, 1914, 2.

21 Ibid.

22 Polly Pry, "Death Horror Hovers over Mazatlan," *Denver Times*, July 22, 1914, n.p.

23 E.g., "Firing Ceases as Polly Pry Visits Rebels," *Denver Times*, July 22, 1914, n.p.; "Yaqui Indians Attack: Polly Pry under Fire," *Denver Times*, July 29, 1914, n.p. Polly Pry Papers, Denver Public Library, Western History Collection.

24 *The Houston Post*, August 6, 1914, 6.

25 Polly Pry, "Colorado Plays Big Part in Defeat of General Huerta," *Denver Times*, July 1914, 12. Polly Pry Papers, Denver Public Library, Western History Collection.

Chapter 13: Lakeshore, Englewood, and Poppies

1 See David Forsyth, *Denver's Lakeside Amusement Park: From the White City Beautiful to a Century of Fun* (Boulder: University Press of Colorado, 2016).

2 E.g., "Coming Summer at Lakes," *Denver Post*, April 30, 1916, 22.

3 "Polly Pry Now an Impresario," *Rocky Mountain News*, April 30, 1916, 6.

4 Ibid.

5 "Casino Company Due Today," *Rocky Mountain News*, June 4, 1916, 9.

6 Letter from A. D. Lewis, President, Tourist and Publicity Bureau of the Denver Civic and Commercial Association, to Leonel Ross Campbell, April 20, 1916. Polly Pry Papers, Denver Public Library, Western History Collection.

7 Letter from Leonel Ross Campbell to Thomas Mohr [spring 1916]. Polly Pry Papers, Denver Public Library, Western History Collection.

8 Casino Theater playbill. Polly Pry Papers, Denver Public Library, Western History Collection.

9 "Mrs. M. E. Campbell Is Called by Death," *Denver Post*, March 12, 1917, 4.

10 "U. S. Red Cross Sends a Call to Polly Pry," *Denver Post*, September 13, 1918, 2.

11 US Passport Applications, 1795–1925, Ancestry.com, Ancestry.com Operations, Inc., 2007, Provo, UT. For unknown reasons, Campbell began putting her place of birth as "Jackson, Missouri" on her travel documents in 1914. There is a Clinton, Missouri, near Jackson; it may be that over the decades she confused this with Clinton, Illinois.

12 "Polly Pry, Back from Albania Relies on U. S. to Secure Its Independence," *Denver Post*, February 13, 1920, 24.

13 "'Polly Pry' Makes Plea for U.S. to Aid Albania," *Rocky Mountain News*, March 3, 1920, 10.

14 Heather Anne Johnson has done a significant amount of research on Madame Guérin and Poppy Day. See https://poppyladymadameguerin.wordpress.com/about-introduction/. "Poppy Demand Exceeds Supply for Special Day," *Rocky Mountain News*, May 23, 1921, 10.

15 This number is extrapolated from city and state newspaper reports. E.g., *The Ottawa Herald* (Kans.), June 3, 1921, 7; *The Daily Ardmorite* (Okla.), May 29, 1921, 9; *Denver Post*, May 30, 1921, 12; *Denver Post*, May 31, 1921, 19; *Salt Lake Tribune* (Utah), June 15, 1921, 17.

16 Letter from Leonel Ross Campbell to Ellis Meredith, July 17, 1922. Polly Pry Papers, Denver Public Library, Western History Collection.

17 E.g., "Come Out to See Movieland," *Denver Post*, January 23, 1918.

18 See, e.g., "Building To House Movie Exchanges Nears Completion," *Denver Post*, October 4, 1922, 12.

19 Letter from Leonel Ross Campbell to Ellis Meredith, July 17, 1922. Polly Pry Papers, Denver Public Library, Western History Collection.

20 "Polly Pry," *Denver Post*, Contemporary Section, February 10, 1968, 6.

21 Ibid.

22 Gayle Shirley, *More Than Petticoats: Remarkable Colorado Women* (Lanham, MD: Rowman & Littlefield), 112–113.

Index

ABOUT THE AUTHOR

Julia Bricklin has authored a dozen articles for well-respected commercial and academic journals, such as *Civil War Times*, *Financial History*, *Wild West*, *True West*, and *California History*. She is the author of the biography *America's Best Female Sharpshooter: The Rise and Fall of Lillian Frances Smith*. Bricklin grew up in southern California, obtained a journalism degree at Cal Poly San Luis Obispo and worked in the TV/film industry for fifteen years before obtaining her master's degree in history at Cal State Northridge. In addition to serving as associate editor of *California History*, the publication of the California Historical Society, she is a professor of history at her local community college. She lives in Los Angeles with her husband and two children.